The Four F's of Leadership

Brigadier General Thomas V. Draude,
USMC (Retired)

Copyright © 2022 by Brigadier General Thomas V. Draude, USMC (Retired)

All rights reserved.

No portion of this book may be reproduced in any form without written permission from the publisher or author, except as permitted by U.S. copyright law.

Contents

Foreword — V

Introduction — VIII

1. Part 1 - Fatigue — 1
   - Physical Fatigue
   - Sleep Is Essential
   - Bad Habits Put Leaders at a Disadvantage
   - Mental Exhaustion
   - Emotions Can Exhaust You
   - Routines and Time Management Optimize Performance
   - Semper Fs: Fighting Fatigue

2. Part 2 - Fear — 25
   - What's More Powerful than Fear?
   - Overcoming Fear
   - Fear Beyond the Battlefield
   - Semper Fs: Fighting Fear

3. Part 3 - Failure — 49
   - What is Failure?
   - Experts on Tap; Leaders on Top

    You Can't Learn from Mistakes If You Don't Discuss Them

    Leaders Own Their Mistakes

    The Road to Hana

    Failure Feels Personal, But It Is Not

    Semper Fs: Figuring Out Failure

4. Part 4 - Feelings   81

    Feelings Mean You Are Human

    The Best Leaders Feel Empathy

    You Can Pretend to Care, But You Cannot Pretend to Be There

    Semper Fs: Feelings are Fundamental

5. Wrapping Up the 4Fs   101

Acknowledgments   104

Foreword

Let me begin with "truth in advertising." I have known Brigadier General Tom Draude since 1962 and he is my dearest friend. He asked me to write this forward but in typical Tom Draude fashion, he demanded that I be absolutely unbiased in my comments. I will do so.

Hundreds of leadership books are published each year. They cover leadership from every angle. Some are promising the "secret sauce" to success; others a "by the numbers" methodology; while others deal with the question of whether leaders are "born or made." All of these books are valuable, and I have read quite a few of them over the years. Each one offers worthwhile advice. General Draude has done something different...he has addressed leadership by discussing it in terms that are critically important but might make some readers uncomfortable.

How many leadership books have been written on the impact of the Four F's of Leadership: Fatigue, Fear, Failure, and Feelings? How many have been written by a former Marine Corps

General who fought in two wars, earned multiple medals for bravery, then went on the serve as the Senior Vice President and General Manager of two USAA regions, then became the President and CEO of the Marine Corps University Foundation, a major non-profit, and then went on to be an adjunct instructor at two major Florida universities? This is not a typical "battlefield to the boardroom" leadership book. It is a book that addresses, head on, the critical issues that can and do impact on leadership...and addresses them from multiple angles based on lessons learned in both the public and private sectors. The 4 F's are insidious and can severely impact a leader and, more importantly, an organization. The better the leader understands these dynamics and how best to overcome them, the greater the chances of his or her success and the success of their people.

General Draude courageously does a deep dive on the 4 F's using his own experiences to highlight the dangers and pitfalls of each. The often-riveting personal examples he uses...of failures and successes...make this book even more valuable and one that deserves a place on any leader's bookshelf. When I read about the 4 F's, I reflected on my own life...public and private...and realized that there were multiple times when I could have used such a valuable book...one that talked of leadership challenges rarely mentioned but often present.

On a personal level, this book is so like Tom Draude. A man of great character who is willing to share significant lessons he learned during his multiple careers and do so with complete openness. A brilliant leader, a superb teacher, a man of great compassion and empathy...all of these are on full display in this remarkable book. I urge each reader to devour the lessons found in this book lest the 4 F's end up devouring the reader.

Charles C. Krulak
General, US Marine Corps (Ret.)
31st Commandant of the Marine Corps

Introduction

Almost 60 years ago I had my first combat experience. In 1965 our battalion was on a "Search and Destroy" operation south of Chu Lai, a US Marine airfield south of Da Nang. I was Executive Officer (XO) of Company "M", Third Battalion, Seventh Marines.

It was another blistering hot day. (I recalled Rudyard Kipling's words in "Gunga Din": "Where the 'eat would make your bloomin' eyebrows crawl…" and there were no Gunga Din's in our ranks). The temptation to find shade was constant, but the shade often hid "booby traps" inflicting wounds or death with nothing to show for it. The challenge was to remain focused despite the fatigue we were enduring and the possibility of contact…at the time and place of the Viet Cong's choosing, not ours.

We were on a sweep with another company when I heard shots fired from our front. I ran to the point and saw the body of Staff Sergeant Benavente who had been killed instantly by a sniper.

He and I had attended Mass so I knew he was a Catholic. I knelt by his body, which had been pulled from the line of fire, said a silent Act of Contrition, and continued on the sweep.

The sniper, two as we learned, were in a thickly covered field about the size of a football field. All eyes were on me as the senior Marine, waiting for my decision.

I told our Vietnamese interpreter to yell to them to surrender. Their response was to fire more rounds in our direction. These were "hard core" Viet Cong who would fight to their deaths.

To charge into the field would be foolhardy and dangerous. The snipers knew which way we were coming, but we didn't know their exact location. Artillery would mean we would need to pull back to a safer location from the cannons' rounds and would take more time, perhaps allowing the enemy to escape.

I decided to flush them out by fire and called up the flame-thrower team and instructed them to set the field on fire. As the flames reached the field's center, one of the enemy snipers threw a grenade...at me! As I followed its trajectory towards me, time seemed to slow down.

I had two thoughts: First, "Can we talk about this? If you got to know me you'd realize I'm a hell of a guy!" Although killing was part of my training, being the target of a stranger trying to kill me was something I had not considered. Second, my training and education had not covered the sensations I was experiencing. I later realized they were normal, but I wish I had been better prepared.

The grenade hit the ground far enough away to not injure any of us. The effect surely focused us even more on the fact that we were not fighting little men in black pajamas armed with antique weapons, but rather trained and well-equipped, worthy adversaries. My respect for them increased significantly and I now had a greater appreciation of the challenges of the French in fighting these men's fathers...and grandfathers...until 1954.

We could now advance into the field which had burned sufficiently for us to see deeper into it. The two snipers were still alive and dangerous and determined to fight to the death. We killed both with gunfire.

I had seen dead enemy Vietnamese and dead Marines in Operation Starlite a few months before. This was the first time I viewed death as a direct result of my actions. I knew there would be more...more than I ever could have imagined. I had chosen a dangerous profession. As a Marine, it was more of a vocation or "calling" than a job, career, or profession.

After that experience, I reflected on this taste of combat. I had experienced feelings and emotions which were never covered in my training. I felt a sense of betrayal because my Marine officer instructors, all veterans of either World War II or Korea, or both, focused primarily on combat tactics, but never imparted any wisdom about actual combat leadership. I wish that the seasoned battle veterans had spent more time with us, offering us the type of wisdom that can only come from experience. They could have told us, for example, "Listen, when you go into combat, here are some things that you're going to experience. You ought to be aware of them beforehand so that when these things hit, you won't say, 'Gee, is this "normal"? How come I'm feeling this way? How come I'm sensing this or that?' You'll be able to take these things in stride, see that the feelings you are having are completely normal, and do a better job."

I vowed that if I survived combat I would never pass up the opportunity to share the things I had learned about Combat Leadership. Over time, I placed them in an easy memory aid of the Four F's: Fatigue, Fear, Failure, and Feelings.

Over the course of my career in and out of the military, I was surprised to learn that leadership in the Marine Corps was applicable to other positions in the world of business, nonprofits and education. This realization propelled me to share my thoughts, experiences, successes, and failures for the benefit of other leaders.

I remember World War II, even though I was very young when it occurred. My dad was a German immigrant too young for World War I and too old for World War II, but very patriotic. That patriotism was instilled in me by both parents. One uncle had served in World War I, and uncles and a cousin served in World War II. In many ways I grew up with war but with no immediate members in the armed services.

One day during World War II we had a visitor...a Marine! This Marine was Vernon Butz, a prominent lawyer who closed his practice and enlisted in the Marine Corps the day after Pearl Harbor. Although I was only 3 or 4 years old at the time, I remember his green uniform and the Black Eagle, Globe, and Anchor Insignia on his blouse and cap. My father, a good friend of Mr. Butz, said "This man is a Marine. He is the best!"

That stayed with me. I knew then what I wanted to be. It was reinforced as I battled a low self-image, that "little fat fellow," as one grade-school teammate's mother once described me. I vowed to become a Marine so no one would hold me in low regard again!

It was my great fortune that the stars aligned and several little miracles unfolded, all leading to my eventual acceptance to the Naval Academy. My teachers and coaches always were supportive, and my dear mother was a constant source of strength. When she died at the start of my second class (or junior year) at the Naval Academy, it was hard not to be bitter. I was just beginning to receive recognition for my accomplishments which would have made her so proud. Suddenly she was gone. Although now in hindsight, as a parent myself, I realize had she been alive during my tours in Vietnam, she would have been in constant torment watching the war on television. She would have imagined me in every scene of death and destruction, every accident, every heartbreaking horror. How many parents, spouses, siblings, children, friends endured that agony? At least my Mom was spared from it.

My Catholic faith has been a major factor in my life and remains so.

When I retired from the Marine Corps, I worried that I would not be prepared for new civilian challenges since there was little demand for the combat skills I had acquired in the civilian world. This is a mistake many military retirees make. We forget that what we can bring to a civilian organization is the strong sense of leadership we learned while in uniform.

So this book is for leaders, military and others. It is my way of sharing aspects of leadership rarely discussed. How does one recognize and react to Fatigue, Fear, Failure, and Feelings?

My hope is that my sharing these lessons will benefit other young and emerging leaders.

Part 1 - Fatigue

The Operation was named "Mallard." I renamed it "Sitting Duck" when I realized how exposed Mike Company was. We had become easy targets in a poorly planned operation near Da Nang. Our Zone of Action in which we operated was surrounded on three sides by water, too deep to wade.

After landing by helicopter I was ordered to lead a reinforced platoon to establish a blocking position at the southern end of our zone, several kilometers from our landing zone. Since we landed late in the day, our movement lasted through the night. Once we were in position, the rest of the company would drive the enemy into our position.

At first light the sweep began, but without much contact. When the company's main body joined us the Viet Cong began their fires...from across the waters. There was no way to attack them on land, and the weather limited any air support. This continued through the day and into the night.

When our company commander, Captain T. G. McFarland was wounded, I assumed command of Mike Company. I remember the shock of seeing him lying on a poncho, coherent but in great pain. Lying nearby was our artillery forward observer, Lieutenant George Lancaster. George was holding his left wrist with his right hand, but his left arm was severed below the elbow. He would not let go of his wrist, almost as if his arm would be healed if he did not let go of it. Both of these fine officers survived. As casualties mounted our focus was on the fight and on their evacuation and resupply of ammunition. Thanks to artillery fires, we were able to accomplish both. I remember making a lot of promises to God that night, praying for the evacuation of our wounded. When there was a lull in the firing I gathered my platoon commanders together to make plans for my second night without sleep. I was truly fatigued and did not permit myself to sit down for fear of losing focus. After not sleeping for over 48 hours and experiencing the mental challenges and the effects of the ebb and flow of adrenaline, I realized how devastating fatigue can be. From that point forward, I paid more attention to fatigue, its symptoms, and how to prepare for it.

• • • ● • ● ● • •

It might seem obvious that a leader should think early and often about fatigue. But surprisingly, it is too often overlooked.

Combat is an exhausting, grueling, and numbing experience that is often worsened by weather and terrain. It is 24/7 with few time-outs or pauses. It is filled with mental, physical, psychological and emotional stress.

Fatigue is not confined to the battlefield or combat training. Fatigue is equally present in our business and home lives. Following my military career, I dealt with intense fatigue during successful treatment for non-Hodgkin's lymphoma, which necessitated debilitating chemotherapy sessions that left me tired, but still determined. I learned that I could push myself when fatigued, as long as I understood that my decisions and reactions were going to be affected. I also learned that eventually I would need to pause from that push. Leaders can "surge" when necessary, but it can't become the "norm." Fatigue is something people brush off, but it's a condition that impacts us more than we realize. As in combat, and in cancer treatment, fatigue can be mental, physical, psychological and emotional. What is important is developing a plan to pace yourself, knowing that you will need to push at times. I have no doubt that the lessons I learned in combat helped me battle through my cancer treatment.

In this next section, I am going to share how to use rest, relaxation, routine and even smart planning to fight fatigue.

Physical Fatigue

Fatigue too often is overlooked as a reason for combat failure on a variety of fronts. Underestimating physical fatigue can lead to burnout and injury. Showing up rested and restored is central to success in many aspects of our work and personal life. In the military, due to the dangerous environments in which we operate, fatigue can often be fatal.

Robert Sumwalt, National Transportation Safety Board vice chairman, reported during a Federal Aviation Association symposium in July 2016 that from 2000 to 2016, fatigue was associated with 250 fatalities in air carrier accidents.[1] Symptoms associated with fatigue include slower reaction times, difficulty concentrating on tasks resulting in procedural mistakes, lapses in attention, inability to anticipate events, higher tolerance for risk, forgetfulness, and reduced decision-making ability.[2]

Physical fatigue can come from simple exertion. But there also exists a passive fatigue that results from the sheer weight of the gear soldiers must carry. Have you noticed how children are often straining under the weight of their backpacks? This is not good for their growing bodies, and puts unnecessary stress on their backs and spines. But it's worse with the military. Marines and Soldiers are supposed to be tough enough to withstand the weight of the gear they carry with almost-superhuman effort.

And of course in the Marines, the very moment you feel you most need to take a break is likely the exact moment that you can't let your guard down. Diligence and focus are vital, despite the fatigue we feel. I have noticed instances where the military world has remained oblivious to this fact. In combat, fighters must be able to move to the point of contact with what they will need to win!

Fatigue remains a serious issue in the military. Research conducted in 2014 by the Army Public Health Center showed that, "soldiers with inadequate sleep suffer from chronic diseases such as hypertension, diabetes, depression, obesity and cancer." This research also showed that soldiers with fatigue suffered "higher mortality rates, lower quality of life and overall less productivity."[3]

When I read S.L.A. Marshall's "A Soldier's Load and the Mobility of a Nation, " I learned that no more than 33% of a combatant's body weight should be carried. Unfortunately, we often demand much more than 33%. We need to determine what is really needed in the pack of a combat Infantryman.

Army and Marine Corps doctrine acknowledges the harmful effects of excessive weight, but in practice historical guidelines for weight limits are not followed. Soldiers have long carried heavy burdens into war, but today's soldiers carry an unprecedented amount of weight. March loads stayed at approximately 80 pounds during Vietnam but grew to 100 pounds afterward, with a maximum march weight over 160 pounds in Grenada in 1983. In Iraq and Afghanistan, march weights have approximated 100 pounds or more."[4]

It was not always this way. The knapsacks and haversacks that the Marines used in World War II, Korea, and even in Vietnam were much smaller than the packs carried today. The logic behind carrying a small pack is simple: the larger the pack, the greater the inclination to stuff more into it. In today's military, we load our Soldiers and Marines with packs that weigh 70, 80, or 90 pounds. This heavy pack adds to the weight of the body armor, weapons, helmet and ammunition they already have on their person. What we are doing to these fighters is almost criminal. They may be willing to fight, but can they fight efficiently while carrying such heavy loads?

While we often have Forward Operating Bases (FOB's) from which patrols or attacks are launched and allow non-essential gear to be left there, establishing those FOB's often requires movement by foot, not helicopters or other means of transportation. The leader determines what is essential for the mission and that will determine the load. The hope is that the leader does not try to pack for every possible contingency!

The deleterious effects of fatigue are too often underestimated, in combat and in everyday life, in work and at home. I know that combat is an exhausting, grueling and numbing experience often worsened by weather and the terrain. But combat goes on... nonstop!

Unfortunately, emotional, mental and physical fatigue are also part of our everyday lives. In a world such as ours today where work and home are often blended, one leads into the other without guidelines for when to work and when to relax. So fatigue has become endemic. Burnout is common. This has been especially so during the Covid-19 pandemic, which upended the work and home lives of millions of people. "Do we now work at home, or live at work?"

My first recommendation is to encourage stronger boundaries between work commitments and home life. That is not always possible, so another recommendation is to take small breaks during the day and focus on something not work-related. This could be as simple as taking 10 minutes to go for a quick walk, call a friend or read a chapter of a book. Oftentimes, a change is as good as a rest.

Sleep Is Essential

The second part of fatigue is the failure to understand the necessity for sleep. When I attended exercises at Twentynine Palms[5] I would routinely see a battalion commander and his staff stay up seventy-two straight hours. Nobody slept. Everybody would be in the fight. It was truly "24/7" for everyone in the command group. After all, we were "essential," right? After 72 hours, they'd declare victory and then everybody would crash. In combat, after 72 hours, you're just getting started. Some commanders failed to understand the necessity for sleep for those around them as well as for themselves. It is a failure not to realize that you have to ensure everyone in the entire unit is as rested as possible.

Studies tell us that if you can get about four hours of uninterrupted sleep, you can function for a foreseeable stretch of time. Four hours is about what it takes to refresh us and allow us to function effectively. Human beings deprived of sleep for 24 hours experience an impairment similar to a blood alcohol concentration (BAC) of 0.10%[6], which is over 25% higher than the legal BAC level to drive in the United States.

Folks used to boast to me, "Well, I've gone 48 hours without sleep." My response would be, "That means that you're operating at a greatly reduced efficiency. That means that you're bringing to bear a fraction of the training, the education, the experience, the knowledge—all of those things that we're counting on you as a leader to have." I was not impressed!

Sometimes you had to be up for 48 hours, but other times it became almost a matter of pride. It was an attitude similar to, "I'm a tougher person than you are because I can drink more." What nonsense. Each of us has different limitations and capabilities, but we all need sleep.

When you do not get sleep, the effects can be devastating. There is a tendency to reverse numbers. If you're a Soldier, Sailor, Airman, Marine, or Coastguardsman, you know the effects that would have on fire-support coordination or navigation when you start reversing numbers on maps or charts. All of these things that so often are a part of fatigue. I recall commanders in the field who have been relieved of their duties because of bad decisions made due to sleeplessness.

In the civilian world, we see the dangerous effects of sleep deprivation as well. The National Transportation Safety Board (NTSB) determined that fatigue (including sleepiness) was the probable cause of 57 percent of crashes leading to a truck driver's death.[7] If that wasn't bad enough, consider the NTSB's finding that for each truck driver fatality, another three to four people are killed.[8]

Americans generally do not get enough rest. We abuse our bodies by depriving ourselves of sleep, and we tell ourselves that we are somehow stronger and tougher by needing less sleep. But this is false. In fact, a recent study[9] showed that adults in their 50s who get fewer than six hours of sleep a night are far more likely to suffer dementia in their 70s than those who regularly slept six or more hours a night. It is not a badge of honor to get by on little sleep! It is a prescription for failure.

Misguided ideas about sleep and strength encourage us to press on regardless of exhaustion. Again, this is a recipe for disaster. Consider that sleep deprivation has been used as a form of torture[10] because of its insidious ability to break the will and muddle the mind, impacting our thinking, our judgment and our focus. Fatigue is more than lack of sleep – it is a sapping of energy that is the result of poor judgment that can lead to even poorer decisions. I learned to spot the signs of fatigue in those I led. When people's behavior shifted, when I spotted slower reflexes or a reduction in focus, I took the necessary steps to ensure they could get rest. As for myself – I know when I am tired because I lose my sense of humor. I have often needed my team to tell me when I have become blind to my own exhaustion and tell me, "Go take a nap, Boss!"

A well-known adage of a World War II infantryman was, "Never stand up when you can sit down; never just sit down when you can lie down; never just lie down when you can sleep!"

Unfortunately, the need to encourage sleep is too often overlooked as an important tenet of good leadership.

When I commanded the Fifth Marine Regiment, I received a visit from the division commander during a command post exercise (CPX)[11] – who asked why Marines were lying outside the combat operations center. I replied that I believed they were asleep. He responded, "I know they're asleep, dammit – but *why* are they asleep?"

"Because they are radio operators who need to be fresh for their next watch," I said. He was not pleased but I knew we needed to practice as we would fight in the future. In fact, I learned to change radio operators to a different task – providing security, maintaining radios and equipment, etc. – so they would remain sharp and focused – especially when dealing with supporting arms where reversing numbers can be deadly, literally!

In Vietnam, I made sure we rotated our radio operators so that they did not get tired. When they got tired, they often became nasty to one another. Nobody needed that. All we were trying to do was communicate and accomplish the mission. You do not need fatigue to muddy the message.

I had the honor, as Assistant Division Commander (ADC), of leading the First Marine Division into Kuwait at the start of Desert Storm.[12] The first day of the war was long with lots of excitement to follow. We were suffering virtually no casualties and I thought we were being led into a "fire sack" between the minefields with no place for cover from enemy artillery fire. At one point well into the next day, the Division Commander, Major General Mike Myatt (Cobra)[13], deemed it was time for me to go take a nap – perhaps he recognized my dwindling sense of humor and other symptoms. I obeyed.

Another instance of dealing with evident fatigue involved one member of our division staff. A lieutenant colonel who was one of our watch officers in Desert Storm became frozen at the map, which he was supposed to be reading so he could advise us of the current situation. He was unable to make a decision. I saw that he was exhausted and could not act as his training and experience had taught him. I could not leave him there in that state, so I quietly pulled him from his position. Careful not to humiliate him during a tense period of the campaign, I told him that we needed him to report to the main command post, which was a less demanding position, farther from the action.

I replaced him with a U.S. Army liaison officer who performed admirably. The Marine lieutenant colonel had, indeed, become exhausted from his role in the theater of war. Freezing and doing nothing can be just as bad as making a poor decision. In other words, he could have caused fatalities by not making a solid decision in time to stave off an enemy advance.

Marines, and other military service personnel, are trained to deal with fatigue – but training can only take you so far. Since the battlefield is intense, trainees are driven to lengths they had not thought possible in order to instill confidence that they are even tougher than they otherwise first thought. Of course, this type of training has to be done by experts, not amateurs, or the results can be devastating. And not all training can prepare trainees for the real circumstances of battle.

Bad Habits Put Leaders at a Disadvantage

Many leaders I knew smoked cigarettes to combat fatigue. The first two times I was in Vietnam I did not smoke. The third time I did. I regret the impact that nicotine had on my body, including nicotine fits that hit in the middle of a firefight! In addition to nicotine dependency, caffeine is also an issue for many soldiers and non-soldiers alike. I have known plenty of people who say, "I can't start operating until I've had three cups of coffee." Well, in combat you are probably not going to have three cups of coffee. I used to tell leaders to quit their addictive habits beforehand – do not smoke, do not chew tobacco, do not become a caffeine fiend. All these things can have an adverse effect in combat because they hurt one's physical structure. It is best to enter combat with as few physical limitations as possible, since the stress and strain of combat will be more than enough to contend with. No one needs the added layer of addiction draining them in combat.

The military is doing a much better job of teaching these lessons now. And of course, these lessons need to be constant throughout life. Just think of how many people have not paid attention to their physical health and are now suffering the consequences. Exercise and sufficient sleep should be the routine we practice, despite the recent challenges of the COVID-19 pandemic.

Complicated and sensitive situations, such as replacing the lieutenant colonel who was fatigued, helped me to become a more observant leader in my post-military career. At USAA and elsewhere, I made it a point to get to know the people around me. By truly knowing the people I was privileged to lead, I could become an even better leader. I could tell when someone was not themself. I found that a quick chat with someone whose behavior concerned me, a quick reinforcement of someone's worth and the work, and even a simple break did wonders not just for individuals, but also for the overall success of entire units.

Mental Exhaustion

Mental fatigue can be as draining as physical fatigue. The sheer weight of being responsible as a leader for your troops can be mentally exhausting, especially when there are no time-outs or let-ups. Knowing the signs of fatigue in yourself and others can help you avoid burnout. Signs might include difficulty concentrating, taking a longer time than usual to make a decision, or simply acting in ways that are outside of your personal norm.

Infantry personnel have many things on their minds. You do not have to be a combat service person to know mental fatigue. People in the workplace are well aware of how exhausting desk work and multiple meetings can be. Statistics on human energy consumption show that about 20% of calories go to the brain.[14] We need a lot of fuel to function properly.

Emotions Can Exhaust You

The reason armed services personnel must meet physical fitness and wellness standards is because combat is physically draining and emotionally demanding. It is easy to ignore the debilitating effects of strong emotions or mental exhaustion. I've learned that being physically fit impacts every aspect of life. Being able to withstand physical demands makes it easier to stay emotionally sound, which leads to better decisions.

The officer plays an important role in preventing fatigue. It is more than simply putting loads on the troops or by understanding there is going to be wear and tear on the body. Effective leaders make sure their team members are in good physical shape; they teach their team that taking care of the bodies also takes care of the minds. *Mens sana in corpore sano*, as the Roman poet Juvenal wrote: "A sound mind in a sound body." These are essential truths: Everyone has to take care of their own body, and in order to do so, everyone must rest.

Office work, and an office atmosphere, as well as long-distance remote work these days, can be taxing to our bodies and our souls.

Routines and Time Management Optimize Performance

Good routines can go a long way toward making you and your work more efficient and less draining. I established routines at the U.S. Naval Academy and maintained them through The Basic School[15] and as a young officer. Both institutions held "reveille" to start the day, which was then filled with formations, meals, instruction, physical activity of one kind or another, and "taps," either mandatory or voluntary. When I retired from USAA,[16] before I led the Marine Corps University Foundation

(MCUF), I had more time on my hands and the previous routines did not fit. What did I do to fill the time and what did I do to keep the train on the tracks? I adjusted as life changed.

Time is the only thing you cannot buy. I have been reminded of this by visiting the Vietnam Memorial in Washington, seeing the engraved names of lives lost. We need to take advantage of the present and use the time we have been allotted in the best way possible. We never know what the future holds.

I learned discipline at home, at high school and at the Naval Academy. I learned to adjust and adapt to different situations – to create routines in order to maximize time and minimize effort, therefore avoiding fatigue.

Later in my military career, as the executive officer of 1st Battalion, 5th Marines, at Camp Pendleton, California, I implemented a routine to make more efficient use of what I jokingly refer to as "the craps of time."

When I first arrived at the battalion, the head – the latrine – was shared by officers and Staff Non-Commissioned Officers in the headquarters. In the toilets (head) was a big table, like a round poker table, on top of which were magazines such as *Playboy, Penthouse, Hustler*—you get the idea. I saw that and said to the police sergeant in charge of the area, "What's all this about?"

He stammered, "Well, sir, you know…"

"No, no," I said. I swept all the magazines off the table. "You get rid of all this crap. I'll provide the magazines."

I started bringing in magazines like *Infantry, Marine Corps Gazette, Naval Institute Proceedings*—professional magazines that would be available there so that when somebody would come in to use the head, grab a magazine and hopefully become engrossed in the article and take the magazine home, and from that increase professionalism.

On seeing these magazines, the police sergeant said, "Sir, what a great idea. I am going to build a magazine rack." So, the magazine rack was built and somebody, I forget who, put up a sign on it that read, "Education through Defecation." It was truly the case!

Then, later, I remember getting all of the lieutenants together and talking about professional reading and them saying they did not have time to read. I said, "Wait a minute. Of course you have time to read. You have to do as Oliver Wendell Holmes once told one of his clerks, 'Young man, make use of the scraps of time.' The scraps of time are those bits of time that are available to us that oftentimes we are unprepared to exploit.

While waiting at the dentist's office, for example, if you don't bring a book, you might end up re-reading a three-year-old copy of Reader's Digest Well, those are the scraps of time. And as one lieutenant who retired as a lieutenant general said, "Now with a library in our head, we make use of not only the scraps of time, but also…the craps of time!"

Semper Fs: Fighting Fatigue

- We all experience fatigue. It is not a weakness or sickness to be cured. It must be recognized and accepted as an issue to be resolved.

- Know your people well, so you can more readily notice their signs of fatigue. This is a leader's responsibility: to know and to care about your people.

- Assess your own patterns to see how you might be adding to the fatigue of your team members and others. Do your choices and actions as a leader undermine everyone else's efficiency? Do they raise the general workload and stress without substantial gains? Are you more concerned about "looking good" rather than "being good"?

- Challenge what you do to determine if the efforts you are expending bring value and lead to specific goals. For example, if you have asked your team members to produce a detailed report for a client meeting taking place in a couple of days, do you know how much time that report actually takes to produce? Do you know the complexities involved in gathering the data for which you asked? Are you aware of the other projects that your team members have in progress? If so, can you reprioritize them? Would clients be pleased to know the pressure you put on your team personnel? And will the report you prioritize have a substantial impact on your goals for that client meeting? In other words: Are you putting the team's time, energy, and resources on what brings the greatest returns?

- Examine work processes. These processes can be confusing or inefficient. They often consume enormous time, zap motivation, and increase fatigue. If your team members are tired, behind or obviously fatigued, ask people what is creating the strain. (Yes, you should ask...and be prepared for the answers that you possibly did not want to hear!) Are there too many layers of review? Is there a lack of communication about what is expected? Are deadlines too short? Is there a lack of resources? Take steps to resolve the conflicts.

- Know yourself and be brutally honest with that assessment of your fitness. Correct your own fatigue-driven deficiencies. Read or consult experts on ways to improve. (Self-improvement includes this aspect of what makes you the person you are. Become better.)

- Here are signs of fatigue to watch for:

    - Loss of humor

- Slowed response time

- Difficulty in making a decision or in concentrating- becoming easily distracted. Yearning for simple tasks requiring less of your time and attention. (I recall the story of an old general who, in the heat of battle, was not leading but rather was firing cannons — this obviously was not his job! Leading was hard, but the general knew how to fire cannons. Are you "firing cannons" when you should be leading?)

- Watch out for these symptoms in yourself and care for yourself. This is not selfishness!

- Staying physically fit minimizes fatigue. Make time to work out and make healthy eating choices. Your brain uses 20% of calories, make sure you are eating properly and enough. Avoid addictions like caffeine and alcohol.

- Establish routines to help optimize your time-the one gift that cannot be replaced! Time wasted is time lost forever! Reflect on your waking moments and energy. What example does your boss set? How about you?

- "Fatigue makes cowards of us all" in the words of a great leader, Coach Vince Lombardi. Fatigue affects the next "F"-Fear!

1. https://www.cnn.com/2009/TRAVEL/05/15/pilot.fatigue.buffalo.crash/index.html
2. Caldwell, John A. (2012). "Crew Schedules, Sleep Deprivation and Aviation Performance". Current Directions in Psychological Science.
3. https://www.army.mil/article/184721/fighting_fatigue_better_soldiers_through_better_sleep
4. "The Soldier's Heavy Load," by Lauren Fish and Paul Scharre, which covers findings of the Center for a New American Security's study on dismounted soldier survivability. This report was in response to a study conducted for the Army Research Laboratory to identify future concepts and technologies to improve soldier survivability and effectiveness over the next 20-30 years in order to identify high-payoff science and technology investment areas.
5. Twentynine Palms is a Marine Corps air-ground combat training center, operated by Camp Pendleton, near Joshua Tree, Calif. The 935-square-mile base is the largest U.S. Marine Corps base and the premier live-fire, combined-arms training facility in the world. Approximately 20,000 active-duty Marines and sailors and their families are stationed at the Combat Center, and more than 50,000 active-duty and reserve Marines and sailors, as well as other U.S. and allied forces, train at the Combat Center 350 days each year.

6. https://www.cdc.gov/niosh/work-hour-training-for-nurses/longhours/mod3/08.html

7. NTSB (National Transportation Safety Board). Safety Study: Fatigue, Alcohol, Other Drugs, and Medical Factors in Fatal-to-the-Driver Heavy Truck Crashes (Volume I). Washington, DC: National Transportation Safety Board; 1990a.

8. NHTSA (National Highway Traffic Safety Administration). Crashes and Fatalities Related to Driver Drowsiness/Fatigue. Washington, DC: United States Department of Transportation; 1994.

9. Findings of the study, supported by the National Institute on Aging (NIA), a part of the National Institute for Health, appeared in Nature Communications, April 20, 2021.

10. Sleep deprivation can be used as a means of interrogation. The United States Justice Department released four memos in August 2002 describing interrogation techniques used by the Central Intelligence Agency. They first described 10 techniques used in the interrogation of Abu Zubaydah, described as a terrorist logistics specialist, including sleep deprivation.

11. A Command Post Exercise (CPX) typically focuses on the battle readiness of staff. It may run in parallel with a field training exercise, or as a stand-alone event for headquarters staff only with heavy emphasis on simulated events.

12. Operation Desert Storm was the combat phase of The Gulf War, which ran from August 1990 to the end of February 1991. Coalition forces from 35 nations, led by the United States, fought Iraq in response to Iraq's invasion and annexation of Kuwait, as a result of oil pricing and production disputes. Operation Desert Shield, which preceded Desert Storm, concerned the build-up of troops and the defense of Saudi Arabia.
13. James Michael Myatt is a retired U.S. Marine major general. He was the Commanding General of the 1st Marine Division in Camp Pendleton, California and in Operation Desert Storm from August 1990 to July 1992. His Call Sign is "Cobra."
14. "In the average adult human, the brain represents about 2% of the body weight. Remarkably, despite its relatively small size, the brain accounts for about 20% of the oxygen and, hence, calories consumed by the body," from "Appraising the brain's energy budget," by Marcus E. Raichle and Debra A. Gusnard, U.S. Library of Medicine, National Institutes of Health.
15. TBS is short for The Basic School, is where all newly commissioned and appointed United States Marine Corps officers are taught the basics of being an "Officer of Marines." The Basic School is at Camp Barrett, Quantico, Va., in the Marine Corps Base Quantico complex.

16. USAA was founded in 1922 by a group of military officers as a mechanism for mutual self-insurance after they were unable to obtain auto insurance because of the perception that they, as military officers, were a high-risk group. Based in San Antonio, TX, USAA is a leading provider of insurance, banking and investment and retirement solutions to 13 million members of the U.S. military and veterans who have honorably served and their families.

Part 2 - Fear

My experience with real fear surprisingly came after my tours in Vietnam.

In the preparation for Operation Desert Storm, I felt fear deeply and personally. My fear was based upon the possible use of Chemical Weapons (CW) by the Iraqi forces in Kuwait. It was reinforced by their defenses in the form of flame trenches, ditches filled with oil and set aflame and set ablaze and minefields in depth to trap us between the mines and destroy us by artillery in their "fire sacks."

As we planned our attack, we kept updating the plan based on information about the Iraqi forces. But the constant was the formidable capability of the Iraqis, the fourth largest land army in the world and veterans of a war with Iran lasting eight years.

Our concerns increased when the Iraqis set fire to the oil fields in Kuwait, plunging the area we would enter in almost total darkness.

I had a lot to fear.

I controlled the fear using the combat experiences I had gained in Vietnam which I shared with the officers and Staff Non-Commissioned officers in the Division, most of whom had no combat experience. My relating the "Four F's" was helpful to them and to me. My hope was to fortify them with a sense of confidence in their ability to lead despite fear.

I was also driven by the memory of Vietnam: how we fought with lots of firepower but little imagination, and lost. I felt blessed that I had that memory and was serving with a few others of my vintage who had "seen that movie before" and wanted a different ending to it.

I translated my concerns by jotting down a few notes for General Myatt, my division commander, on Military Deception. What, if anything, was being planned for this way of "fighting smart?" He forwarded my notes to General Boomer, the First Marine Expeditionary Force (IMEF) commander over all Marines in Desert Storm, who then designated me as the IMEF Deception Officer.

I now had relief for some of my fears. We would save Marine lives by deceiving the Iraqis. I had been tormented by a scene from the movie "Gallipoli" in which soldiers were sacrificed by generals too far from the action to make a difference. Now, as head of deception in addition to serving as the assistant division commander, I possessed the authority to have a larger effect on our outcome.

My relief was not complete, however; I had to display and convey confidence during the days before the assault into Kuwait. I was doing a lot of serious praying at night with my rosary in my sleeping bag.

Fear, recognized but controlled and focused, had become for us an asset, not a liability. My fear of losing lives in the war drove me to seek innovative opportunities for deception.

In order to trick the Iraqis into thinking we were going to launch an amphibious assault, we allowed the media to cover rehearsals of amphibious assaults. Upon seeing this in the news, the Iraqis deployed 5-7 divisions to Kuwait's coast, but we didn't assault the coast. In order to lull the Iraqi defenders of the minefields into a sense of complacency, we broadcasted tank noises every night for a few weeks but didn't attack, so when we did assault them, they were conditioned to hear tank noises with no consequences. We also dropped leaflets urging the Iraqis to surrender–and they did–by the thousands.

My greatest fear in combat was not of dying or being wounded. It was that I might not be the leader my Marines deserved, the one they needed. Every Marine I had lost in Vietnam caused me to ask, "What could I have done to avoid his death? Was his death my fault?" The questioning comes after the action since leaders must stay focused on the situation at hand. But later the examination took place for me. It still does.

Post Traumatic Stress Disorder (PTSD) is now receiving the attention it deserves. It is, I believe, often enhanced by "Survivors' Guilt"...why am I alive instead of my friend, my Comrade. "Why was I spared?"

Fear, for me, was the never ending "Fear of Failure" in combat. Everyone in combat experiences fear of some kind.

Many Marines – and most people outside of the armed forces – are uncomfortable talking about fear. But experiencing fear is the most natural thing in the world when you are in a life or death situation. We have evolved over the course of tens of thousands of years to react to primal fear from unknown or known risks – and we carry that with us in modern times. When we face danger, our thoughts can get sharper, our reactions quicker; but also, fear can freeze us and hold us back.

My ability to face fear also is aligned with what I consider one of my strongest assets: my Catholic faith. For me, Psalm 91 helped me in Desert Storm. It says, among other things, "I will say of the Lord, He is my refuge and my fortress," and "Thou shalt not be afraid for the terror by night; nor for the arrow that flieth by day." Reciting and recalling words from my spiritual life was how I handled most of my fears. But deep down I believed that if I were to be killed I eventually would receive salvation.

Just as important, I did not want to let down my Marines; I wanted to be the officer and commander they needed and deserved.

When I was growing up, I was not good enough to make the Little League baseball team. I was crushed when I had to give my uniform to another player who was a better catcher. But during the off season, I worked my butt off and made All Stars the next year. The feeling of "not being good enough" constantly drove me. I had to do what was necessary to please my parents. I also had to satisfy the drive that I had and to counteract the fear of failure with academics and athletics. Whatever the challenge, I wanted to succeed. It was an awesome responsibility to have the lives of Marines in my hands. So there was a personal requirement for me to be the best officer that I could be.

In my middle age, I was diagnosed with cancer. My reaction was not so much fear but anger: how could this body that I had taken reasonably good care of betray me? So, with that came the image that this was a fight, and I was going to fight this cancer. I was going to win it with the help of the doctors, nurses, chemotherapy and family, but this threat was not going to kill me!

When I told each one of my children that I had cancer, I said, "I'm going to die, but it's not going to be from cancer!" In every battle in life we should fight all the way and then leave the rest in God's hands. With the "Our Father" prayer, we say "Thy will be done." On this occasion I had a chance to really mean it.

"Leaders are dealers in hope," is a quote often attributed to Napoleon. I believe this. Hope can help you face fear, and hope is a powerful weapon for anyone confronting a challenge.

Fear exists not only on the battlefield but in all areas of life. During the Covid-19 pandemic, for example, fear of falling sick, dying, having loved ones die, losing one's job, and so forth tormented and continues to threaten many people. I believe that at some point over the last couple of years many of us have felt a measure of pandemic-related fear. We did not know what would happen to us or those around us.

There are countless other "everyday" fears too, of course: fear of public speaking, heights, failure, success, strangers – the list is endless.

This chapter shares my experiences in working with fear – my own – and the fears of the people with whom I worked and had the privilege to lead. It can be a challenge to overcome the feeling of fear in yourself and in the people you lead. But I have found that you can feel fear without being frozen by it. Remember, it is normal to feel fear. Courage is doing what is required despite the fear.

What's More Powerful than Fear?

Marines do not tend to talk about fear. Instead many Marines believe they are impervious to fear. But we all have self-preservation in our systems – Marines or not – and fear triggers a preservation response. If we did not have an urge to preserve ourselves, we would be in real trouble. The shock that someone is trying to kill you is something that has protected humankind throughout our evolution. It still protects us – but in most situations you have to get past it to move forward.

Before we would go into battle, I would try to prepare the Marines under my command for what to expect. I would try to get them to understand the nature of fear – and how to respond to it.

When I spoke to troops about fear, I led them in question-and-answer sessions, in a semi-Socratic way, to get them to understand how to deal with fear. So, I would ask the troops things such as, "What emotion is stronger than fear?" I'd get an answer such as, "Anger."

I would then say, "Well, anger — that's when you have a flashpoint you've got to control and so forth. That's not stronger than fear. What else?"

Then someone would say, "Revenge."

I'd reply, "Well, revenge is kind of the same mode as anger. That's not stronger than fear. What else?"

I would wait for a while and then I would hear a small voice somewhere pipe up among the audience – obviously the voice of someone who did not want to be recognized. That voice would say, "Love."

I would say, "Exactly!" Everyone would look at each other, puzzled. Love?

Like fear, love is a four-letter word that you do not hear very often in the Marine Corps. But love is what overcomes fear. This is not a new concept, but for a lot of us it is still something of a discovery, because love – or the bonds of affection and companionship – could be the last thing you might think of when you consider people in battle.

But it is powerful, and history has proved that.

During the Battle of Iwo Jima,[1] a new platoon commander named Robert Humphrey[2] cautioned his Marines to stay alert at night because the Japanese might sneak into Marines' lines and kill them. His veteran platoon sergeant reminded him that these Marines had been through so much that they did not care about themselves anymore, but they still cared about their buddies. Taking a cue from the sergeant, the platoon commander called his Marines together and said, "Marines, you need to stay alert tonight or the Japanese will sneak into our lines, and kill your buddies!" Problem solved. Love of the guy on your right and left and a feeling of responsibility for their well-being overcame the fear.

I have my own experience of how the example set by others can help offset fear. One corpsman, "Doc" Richard Lewis, was the bravest guy I ever saw in Vietnam. But when we first went into combat, he said he could not move. He knew he had to move forward. He could not move. He absolutely was petrified. He looked up and saw First Lieutenant Draude moving. I was the company Executive Officer at the time. He told me later that he thought to himself, "Geez, if Lieutenant Draude can do his job, I guess I can do mine." With that, he snapped out of it.

While this corpsman was frozen in fear, I actually was not thinking of anything other than what I had to do. My own self-preservation was not high on the list (and neither was fear). The leader really has the luxury of thinking about other things and other people. For me, the most frightened guy on the battlefield would be the private who has nobody else about whom to worry. The key is to surround everyone with his comrades. Tasks that must be done as a team help control the fear.

One of my heroes spoke about this too. James Mattis[3] has had a long and illustrious career. After I gave my "Four Fs" talk (on which this book is based) to his officers and staff non-commissioned officers (SNCOs), he asked me to come back and give the talk to his Non-Commissioned Officers, Corporals and Sergeants. At another point, he spoke about his own affection for his Marines and touched on the *esprit* of the Corps, such as fighting for your buddies.

"We all know that earning the trust and respect of your subordinates is critical," Mattis said in the interview.[4] "You simply have to earn that trust, you have to earn that respect, every day. Because when it's all over and done with, you're not going to win any fights as a leader – your troops are going to win those fights," he said.

"But there was another word I learned to prioritize as I evaluated units," Mattis added. "And that word was 'affection.' It is not 'being popular.' With all the favoritism that comes with trying to be a popular person as a leader – that is a road to failure. But affection that you create in any unit can be so strong that the troops will stick by one another. They'll carry out the mission, even in peril," he said.

"I bring this one up," Mattis continued, "because I believe that that kind of affection brings out self-discipline — where people don't want to let down the unit. If there is one lesson I learned along the way, it's that the more you can build that kind of affection in a unit — when the going gets tough- when people are getting shot down around you – it'll pull together and it'll be a lot smoother organization. It will move more rapidly and fluidly against the enemy, and it will, generally speaking, lead to you having fewer disciplinary problems."

Overcoming Fear

You must face fear and control it. There are means to do so.

During the Battle of Okinawa, the writer William Manchester[5] received a minor wound that took him out of action. This was referred to as "a million-dollar wound," because it took the serviceman out of combat and also could be an honorable ticket home.

But when Manchester learned that his unit was going into the attack without him, he left the hospital without permission, rejoined his unit. He once again was wounded; this time much more seriously.

Manchester returned to combat because he needed to be with his buddies. He wrote that he could not live with himself if he was not with them during the attack. Even though he was hurt much worse the second time, he did not regret his actions. Not acting on behalf of people he had grown close to was unthinkable to him.

In his book *"Men Against Fire,"* Brigadier General Samuel Lyman Atwood (SLA) Marshall, a military journalist and historian, recounts his research about the U.S. Army in the Pacific during World War II. He was amazed to learn that fewer than 25% of infantrymen fired their weapons in combat. With only one out of four men actively firing, how could their units survive and still win? What were the other 75% doing?

The non-firing infantrymen did not run. They stood firmly at their buddy's side; the troops who did all the shooting were provided presence and comradery by those who could not shoot.

So why do people fight? They do not fight for their country, their Corps, motherhood, apple pie, Sally Lou, or Lost Overshoe, Iowa! They fight for their buddies. Therefore, as a leader you want your Marines to quickly bond and establish the camaraderie that is vital in combat. Replacements need to be bonded as soon as possible in the unit. A good Marine combat unit has no "FNGs"[6] who get harassed and ridiculed, as in that atrocious movie "Platoon." Leaders have a responsibility to place new troops in situations where there are Marines close to them until they have bonded. We fight for our buddies!

Just as with the Marines' reluctance to talk about fear, many military leaders are also hesitant to discuss it because leaders are stereotypically "fearless." Wrong! Leaders also are human beings with the same feelings as everyone else.

In my experience in Vietnam, although fear was all around us, we Marines depended on each other, and we depended on the Vietnamese with whom we worked. So our genuine fears were mitigated. We fight for our buddies!

Simon Sinek, the British-American author, has spoken and written about how great leaders can inspire action. He gave a noted TEDTalk about this. In short, he says that great leaders and organizations focus on *WHY* they do what they do, instead of WHAT they do and *HOW* they do it. This is important for the non-combat leader: you get results when you all know what the *WHY* of your organization is, and the *WHY* of every project. Too many times, people believe they are overwhelmed by paperwork or tasks that seem to make no sense. A leader's job is to make sure that the work that people do makes sense and is meaningful — i.e., the *WHY*.

Viktor Frankl, author of *Man's Search For Meaning*, wrote, "If you can explain the 'Why?', most people can live with the 'How?'."

Identifying my "Why" (accomplishment of the mission and taking care of Marines) is what enabled me to overcome fear in combat. Strenuous preparation and intense focus were my "How."

Fear Beyond the Battlefield

Different forms of fear can surface in everyday life. For a former military professional it could arise in situations where you are not facing the enemy as such, but dealing with the responsibilities of your position. The fear that your best might not be good enough (known these days as "Imposter Syndrome") or the fear that you might let down those you are privileged to lead might in fact be your newest challenges.

After my retirement from the Marine Corps, I joined USAA. In a few years, I became the senior vice president of the SouthEast Region. On the morning of September 11, 2001, I was in our Tampa office when our country was attacked. Many people in the building were watching the terrible events unfold on TV. Other employees were listening to it. It was a devastating situation, made worse by us not knowing who attacked us and why. We all wondered where else we might be attacked and what we were going to do about it.

I first announced on the office loudspeakers what I knew at the time to reduce rumors. Then I moved out on the floor talking to people and reassuring them that our government was going to act quickly. I urged our employees to hang in there. I was asked by higher headquarters if I had activated my emergency action response team (people who had been designated to form an "action committee," for disasters and such). I had not, and I guess that was because I did not think there was a need for it. There was no threat to Tampa that we knew of, and I did not want to fuel the existing fear. I immediately encouraged all employees with children being released from school to leave the office so they could pick up their children, or meet them at home. The right place for our employees was at home with family, not with us at USAA.

On that day I realized that we were now at war again, but I would not be a part of it. Vietnam and Desert Storm were behind me and I was retired. What could I do to help? The first priority was to ensure my employees were safe. By doing so, USAA was doing its part for the men and women and their families who were now at war. Our employees were well trained. We had already, years earlier, instituted a course for our new employees, "Military 101", that helped them to assist our service members and their families. Terms such as "unaccompanied tour" and Permanent Change of Station (PCS) orders, life changing events for those in military service and their families, were known to our representatives who answer calls from our members. In their own way, our representatives were also "in the fight" and proud to be so!

Uncertainty can generate fear. And many people who worked with me that day were fearful not only about their own safety, but the safety of people they knew and the safety of their country. Even the reassuring words from a leader — who himself might be afraid — can do a lot to help people put aside that fear and to concentrate on getting through the day.

What do you do when your fears come to pass?

I am claustrophobic. I realized it in the most dramatic and embarrassing way. Part of my cancer treatment involved Positive Emission Tomography (PET) scans which required me to be flat on my back under a machine for 30 minutes or so without any movement. My first scan was a disaster! I made the mistake of opening my eyes and seeing metal a few inches from my face. I withstood it for as long as I could. Then, in as dignified a way as I could muster, I ordered the poor technician to, "Get me the hell out here!"

No amount of logic or pleading from the technician helped. I wanted out now! Needless to say, I was embarrassed as a combat Marine. I could lead in combat and jump out of airplanes...but I could not handle a procedure that so many others could.

I knew that as a cancer victim, I would end up in or under machines for PET scans or other tests. I had to figure out how to deal with this fear.

I resolved this by anticipating the tests and visualizing my being at ease and completing the exam without drama! I would visualize the room, the machine, the control room, the technicians, all that I could remember from the first PET scan experience. It helped to have a towel over my eyes, but I would keep my eyes shut anyway, just in case. This worked on all successive PET scans along with a little help from saying multiple rosaries.

I am a great believer in visualization and have used it often. The first time was before a briefing to the then new Commandant of the Marine Corps when he visited Marine Forces Pacific when I was in charge of personnel. Before the briefing I pictured the conference room, the faces of those in attendance, the texture of the pointer I would use, and the smells of the area to make my visualization as realistic as possible. Then I continued in my mind's eye to deliver a superb presentation, brilliantly answering the few questions asked because my presentation was so thorough, and hearing the Commandant say it was one of the best briefings on personnel he had heard! Thus, the real presentation is just an "instant replay" of what I had visualized.

This experience and success convinced me that visualization could be pow- erful. I even visualized our success in the Deception Plan in Desert Storm and in the relatively safe movement through the minefields.

Semper Fs: Fighting Fear

- Putting others ahead of ourselves helps mitigate fear. The "luxury of command" is not a nicer fighting hole, a corner office, or better rations. It is thinking about someone else. Leaders establish a culture of trust which reduces uncertainty. Reducing uncertainty reduces fear. Good parents realize this. In an emergency, children look to their parents, whom they trust for clues on how to react. If parents are calm, the children follow that example. Attend to your communications; don't forget that the words, the volume of those words, and the emotion you display are all part of the message you as a leader send.

- Teams support and protect their members, especially during times of strife or challenge, in order to mitigate fear. Good leaders create a culture that encourages support among the team.

- Fears that are part of our daily lives, such as public speaking, can be minimized by visualizing a successful outcome. By doing so, you can build your visualization "muscle." The real experiences often become "instant replays" of the outcomes you visualized.

- Consider all the outcomes you have feared in the past. How many of them were realized, especially to the extent you feared? When they were realized, you have received an inoculation vaccine that makes you less susceptible to fearful outcomes. You survived and can now deal with the "known enemy."

Author, Kankakee, IL, 1950

Author, USNA Commissioning, 1962

Author, Newsweek Aug 1, 1966.
Photo by Michel Renard

Author, Desert Storm, 1991.
Photographer unknown

Author, Official photo for the Presidential Commission on the Assignment of Women in the Armed Forces, 1991-1992.

Author, Photo by Todd L Chappel for the Tampa Tribune, 1999

Author, Guy Wyser-Pratte and John Hales, Marine Corps University Foundation, 2006, Photographer un-known

Mary Campagna (author's Mother-in-law), Author, Ryan Draude, Patrick Draude, Marysandra Draude, Loree Draude, Prince of Wales Room at the Hotel Del Coronado, May 1991. Photographer unknown

1. The Japanese island of Iwo Jima was the site of a memorable battle during World War II. It lies 750 miles south of Tokyo, in the Pacific. In the Battle of Iwo Jima, which ran from February 19 to March 26, 1945, the United States Marine Corps and Navy landed on and eventually captured the island from the Imperial Japanese Army.

2. Robert Humphrey (1923-1997) was a veteran of the battle of Iwo Jima, who went on to become an expert in conflict resolution, based on his wartime and overseas experiences. Humphrey believed that universal values controlled human behavior, and in his work he emphasized a moral, physical, artistic and mental approach to resolving conflicts. In his book, "Values for a New Millennium," he explored ways to reduce violence and to promote cross-cultural harmony.

3. James Mattis is a retired United States Marine Corps four-star general who served as the 26th U.S. Secretary of Defense from January 2017 to January 2019. During his 44 years in the Marine Corps, he commanded forces in the Persian Gulf War, the War in Afghanistan, and the Iraq War (during Desert Storm he was First Battalion, Seventh Marines).

4. On Leadership Lessons," posted Oct 13, 2016, https://www.americanrhetoric.com/speeches/jimmattisonleadershiptraining.htm

5. William Manchester (1922- 2004) was an American author, biographer, and historian. He was the author of 18 books, including, among others, "American Caesar: Douglas MacArthur 1880–1964" (1978), "The Last Lion" (1983, 1988, 2012) a trilogy about Winston Churchill, and "Goodbye Darkness: A Memoir of the Pacific War "(2002).

6. FNG is an abbreviation for "Fucking New Guy," a derogatory term for newcomers, that became popular within combatants of the U.S. Army and the U.S. Marine Corps deployed to South East Asia during the Vietnam War.

Part 3 - Failure

It was April 1966 and I was commanding Mike Company in "Operation Hot Springs" near Da Nang. In our zone of action was a hamlet which seemed peaceful...until it wasn't.

We were hit with mortar and automatic weapons fire as we approached it. I ordered the company to take cover as I directed artillery and air support on it. There was no effect.

The sun was going down and I did not want to face both the enemy and darkness, so I gave the order "Fix Bayonets!" When that order was received, it had an amazing effect on my Marines. There was no chatter, no sound except the "click" of the bayonet on their M-14 rifles. It was as if we sensed that we were about to engage the enemy, not with artillery, mortars, or air. We were about to engage him in close combat, slashing or beating him to death. In a few minutes, someone, at one end of the rifle or the other, would be dead.

That attack was successful and we seized the hamlet. As we were setting in our defensive positions for the night, I was informed that one of my squad leaders, Corporal Frederick W. Miller, from Berlin, Ohio, had been killed. His body was outside our lines.

My Marines were exhausted and now had to dig in their positions. I was determined that Corporal Miller's body be recovered. I instructed my Executive Officer, Lieutenant Jerry White, to set in the company as I went out to retrieve the body.

The following day I was visited by my battalion commander who was surprised to see blood on my flak jacket. I explained what had happened the night before. He was not pleased with me. "Don't ever do anything like that again! Do you understand me?"

I thought, "If I remain silent, it will infer my obedience to his order. But if I remain silent, I will have to live with it for the rest of my life."

So I took a deep breath and responded, "Sir, I understand your order but I could never leave behind a dead or wounded Marine."

He went ballistic and began to relieve me of my command. All of my boyhood dreams of remaining an officer of Marines were over. One does not survive being relieved in combat in the Marine Corps.

As this was happening, a helicopter arrived and out of it jumped the assistant division commander of the First Marine Division (ironically, the same position I would hold in Operation Desert Storm in 1990-1991). As he was walking toward us, I thought, "Come on, God! My dreams are shattered and now a brigadier general is here to grab whatever is left of my ass!' He instead grabbed my hand and began pounding me on my back while saying, "That was great, captain! That was fantastic!" Then he turned to the battalion commander and said, "With company commanders like this, how can you go wrong?"

So instead of being relieved, I received my first Silver Star Medal...after failing in the eyes of my battalion commander! Strange how failure in the view of one senior is viewed as a success in the view of another. Sometimes Failure, like Beauty, is truly in the eyes of the beholder.

What is Failure?

Like fatigue and fear, failure is part of our human nature. How do you handle failures in your juniors? What do you do about your own failures? Or how do you address failures among peers? Failure is a wide-ranging sensation. Sometimes it is based on your own sense of what has gone wrong. It could also be based on a misreading of what you have done or what you believe others have done. Often failure is simply an error writ large. Of course, sometimes failure can be a serious breach of conduct or trust. Failure may be a question of a bad decision or a faulty character. Finally failure can sometimes be a matter of perception.

My definition of failure is not accomplishing a mission or task.

Because the bulk of my experience has been in the military — for the most part — I will address failure as I saw it or experienced it during my career as a Marine.

The Tet Offensive led to a general perception of U.S. failure in Vietnam, while it actually was not an American failure. The Tet offensive was a major escalation in the Vietnam War and one of its largest military campaigns. It began on January 30, 1968, when the forces of the Viet Cong (VC) and the North Vietnamese People's Army of Vietnam fought the forces of the South Vietnamese Army of the Republic of Vietnam (ARVN), the United States Armed Forces and other allies of South Vietnam. This campaign comprised a series of surprise attacks against military and civilian command and control centers throughout South Vietnam. The North Vietnamese hoped that Tet would lead to a general uprising throughout the country to overthrow the South Vietnamese government. Instead, the Viet Cong were virtually eliminated. Yet, the American people perceived that Tet was this brilliant Viet Cong and North Vietnamese success. This perception became the major cause for the United States' eventual withdrawal, and the U.S. failure in Vietnam.

The perception of failure is hard to shake. For example, before the Tet Offensive, General William Westmoreland[1] had said, "We're seeing the light at the end of the tunnel."[2] When you crave success you can fall into the trap of seeing success or positive indicators when they don't actually exist. Maybe the positive indicators that Westmoreland was looking at were what he wanted (ordered) waged: we were killing an increasing number of the enemy. But there was also a dramatic contrast between his view and sudden major battles taking place throughout the country. This difference started the shift in the attitude of the American people. There was a perception of failure rather than success.

Increased bombings and the further incursion of Cambodia, reinforced this belief of failure. From a military standpoint, these actions were the right thing to do. But because the Americans felt they had been deceived—that our forces were not bombing Cambodia, that our forces were not in Cambodia, et cetera—their confidence in the American government was eroded further. Following these actions came a whole raft of incidents that further chipped away at the American public's confidence in its government and military. There arose a general sense of failure in the country. U.S. leaders had lost the credibility of most Americans.

Vietnam tested Americans' patience. People were aware that World War II had not lasted as long as U.S. forces fought in Viet- nam. In Korea, while the United States settled a cease fire, the American people did not consider it a failure. The U.S. natural impatience can be both a liability and an asset. At times, impatience is a liability when Americans want it fast and perfect. When an action is not delivered as expected there's a tendency to say,

"Well, this is a failure. Move on to something else." Too many times it seems Americans do not have the patience to see some things through.

If leaders manage expectations in an unrealistic manner and the results are not what was desired, the feeling of failure is more pronounced. This must be balanced with the desire for optimism expected of leaders. The need to have advisors who truly speak "truth to power" is contrary to popular belief. The public can handle the truth; what they resent is lies or hubris.

Sometimes leaders set themselves up for failure by a "can-do" attitude that can exceed their capabilities or their unit's. For the most part we all strive to be "team players," willing to do what is necessary to get the job done. However, over-promising and under-delivering serve no one. Military leaders are prone to be upbeat and positive, and this can conflict with the reality of the situation. It takes moral courage to tell the boss that the effort is just not working and needs a correction — or termination. Is this a failure? In fact, it can be a worse failure to continue on a course that is not headed toward success.

Experts on Tap; Leaders on Top

We all make mistakes. I have had my share of mistakes – or, if you want, failures. When I took command of my first platoon at Camp Pendleton in 1963, I thought my moment had finally arrived. My boyhood dreams were about to be realized.

Two corporals joined us who had both just come from the drill field in San Diego. They had been reduced in rank from sergeant to corporal for maltreating recruits. Their failures were non-adherence to regulations. These men were a couple of salty individuals, but they also were good Marines. Both Marines turned out to be very good — once I figured out how to work with them.

I received some useful seasoning from the time I spent supervising my platoon sergeant–a Korean War and World War II veteran, who had received the Silver Star Medal in Korea, and who was, unfortunately, also an alcoholic.

As might be expected, I, the new second lieutenant, and the new platoon sergeant, were often at odds.

When we'd prepare for inspection I would go through – in great detail – all that I wanted done. The platoon sergeant already knew what had to be done. And all that I really had to tell him was, "We have an inspection coming up. I'll do an inspection beforehand." But I turned out to be the one doing all of the pre-inspection work. And the platoon sergeant ended up standing there with his arms crossed. I was doing everything that he should have been doing. In effect, I was creating an atmosphere that could lead to failure.

It took a wiser person than I, the company executive officer, to tell me, "Make use of the expertise that you have – and let him do his job." This experienced war veteran staff sergeant was familiar with weapons employment, leading small units, and keeping things in order. I was ignoring all of that because I used the learning I had acquired at The Basic School. I should not have disregarded what I had learned, but I was not tempering that knowledge with the practical experience of this individual and what he had to offer. It is tempting to simplify our leadership positions by categorizing our juniors according to their strengths and weaknesses. Good leaders understand and accept that their jobs are to make the best use of their juniors, mitigating weaknesses, while helping to correct them, and maximizing strengths.

An early-career leadership lesson I learned was that nobody is perfect and nobody is "all bad." The role of the leader is to determine which things people are good at, and let them do them. At times you watch people fail and let them learn. I also believe that one of the great leadership traits is to leave junior leaders alone unless a disaster looms. Retired Army General Pete Dawkins wrote a superb article, "Freedom to Fail," in *Infantry Magazine* in September/October 1965, which should be required reading for all leaders.

You Can't Learn from Mistakes If You Don't Discuss Them

It is important to understand why failure takes place. Often it is because people are trying too hard, or because they are fatigued and/or fearful. What happens then?

When I was in Amphibious Warfare School[3] I remember the scenario with the fictional Golf Company[4] commander. In the narrative, the entire battalion was ordered to cross the line of departure at a certain time. All the Marines crossed except Golf Company. Students were asked, "What do you do about the Golf Company?"

Some of my classmates said, "Relieve him."

I thought, "Good God. Is this what we've come to where the solution to any problem is relieving? What's going on in the Golf Company? Shouldn't we at least investigate to learn what happened?"

With the knee-jerk reaction of "relieve him" in mind, I made this issue my thesis topic years later at the Army Command and General Staff College in Fort Leavenworth, Kansas. It was 1975 and I was a major.

My premise was that leaders are relieved from their commands when they fail to accomplish the mission. What I learned was that mission accomplishment often had little to do with why people are actually relieved. They are more often relieved because of bad luck, bad press, and sometimes as a result of simple stupidity. It was a good exercise for me to discover what went through the minds of leaders as they determined when a commander should be relieved.

To gather information for the thesis, I asked fellow students and other officers: "When do you relieve a commander?" Several senior officers responded similarly, saying "What a dumb question. If you have to ask that question then you shouldn't be a commander." I found it interesting that because my subject was so controversial many faculty members resisted mentoring me. After all, who wants to support a student writing a thesis on failure?

One faculty member did stand up and became my sponsor. God bless Army Colonel Ben Abramowitz. He became my Rabbi, and said, "This is something we ought to pursue." He provided sound advice and great recommendations.

It bothered me that so many reliefs took place in Vietnam. It became almost a new culture of the military: if a mistake was made, the solution was to relieve the person who made it.

My thesis looked at some of the things that ought to be considered before relieving a commander. It is not part of the current education process, but it should be. The concepts of training and education are different. Training is preparation for certainty; education is preparation for uncertainty. Leaders must be prepared for both!

If the mistake is absolutely egregious or can clearly be defined as a matter of moral turpitude, then relief is in order. If neither of these is the case, first consider the effect a relief would have on the unit. Is there a good replacement available and can that replacement start in a timely fashion?

If you do not have somebody standing in the wings that you can fill in or move up to next in command, then maybe the smart thing to do is to not effect a relief at that time.

You also need to ask, " What's the impact on the mission?" Too often I found that mission accomplishment and the residual impact on the unit were not considered. I discovered that the relief process was often a standard operating procedure: If you screwed up, you "packed up." And only later would the higher-ups look around and ask, "Okay, who do we have to put in this newly created vacancy?"

With a unit in combat the approach just described should not be employed. You have to give more thought. If a person has betrayed you, lied to you, or done something else to cause you to lose absolute confidence, then that person must go. On other occasions, you must consider the following: "What is best for the unit?"

History has many lessons to teach. For example, we can look at General Dwight D. Eisenhower's approach to General George S. Patton during World War II. There were a number of occasions when Eisenhower[5] could have relieved Patton[6] but he did not. Eisenhower saw the larger picture. He knew the notorious slapping incidents[7] certainly damaged troop morale, but there were good reasons to keep Patton in his post. Each time Eisenhower would reach for the phone to relieve Patton, he would say to himself, "Who do I have better at killing Nazis than Patton?" Knowing he had no replacement, he kept Patton in pace. When the fighting was over and Patton said, "The Nazis were kind of like Republicans and Democrats," Eisenhower relieved him. At this time Eisenhower did not need Patton anymore to kill Nazis.

Upon surveying my classmates, I realized that there was a revolving door in Vietnam: routinely in just a one year tour, an Army captain might have on average five different battalion commanders. One after the other serving six months in command, or being relieved every few months. I concluded that you could not have any kind of continuity or focus or unity of command when you have the turmoil of constantly changing commanders. Failure, or its perception, was adding to the leadership turmoil.

In my thesis, I strongly recommended against "instant relief" for mistakes. To quote from my thesis:

"The Vietnam-produced attitude of relieving those who made mistakes would prove a disaster in many cases. The scarcity of replacements would be aggravated by the fast-moving action on the battlefield, which would hinder if not preclude flying in replacement commanders.

The bold imaginative leadership required in a conflict in which we could be outnumbered and outgunned will not exist in a relief-oriented command. Few commanders can exercise such leadership when they view their seniors as men who will tolerate no mistakes and who will 'solve' problems by relief. Commanders must be able to operate in an environment of special trust and confidence. Bold, aggressive, imaginative leadership is nurtured by this atmosphere. Mediocrity and defeatism are nurtured by its alternative."

Early on in my career I made it a point to think of failure as an opportunity. My goal was to allow my Marines to make mistakes. I tried to give them the freedom to fail, except in those cases that demonstrated egregious poor judgment. As a result, I believe that we became a better unit using this approach. Mistakes are not total failures if you learn from them. (President Kennedy once said, "We all err. It's not a mistake until we fail to learn from it")

It is key to never lose confidence in yourself. No one wants a leader who walks around with his head down and a defeated attitude. As one Judge Advocate General (JAG)[8] colonel reminded me, "We all have good days and bad days. On the good days you automatically will not be promoted or get a medal. On bad days you should not condemn yourself forever. Be a leader."

Leaders Own Their Mistakes

Throughout my career, I learned from my mistakes and urged others to learn from theirs. Such an approach can set you up to be considered a failure here and there because you're willing to take the risks to teach, learn, and gain experience.

When I was leading the 5th Regiment, one of the things I found most fulfilling was the opportunity for me to have a direct impact on the development of officers and senior non-commissioned officers (SNCOs). I did this most by showing up. I would spend time with my Marines in the field by holding officer education sessions, by engaging the SNCOs, and letting them know what I expected of them and their roles in helping me develop junior officers.

The SNCOs, the staff sergeants, the gunnery sergeants, first sergeants and master sergeants, and sergeants major and master gunnery sergeants—and all of their valuable experiences, could help the young officers become better professionals. I tried to impress upon them the importance of the roles they had in this effort and urged them to work with me in that regard.

Let me share a story to get the point across.

On one of the exercises at Twentynine Palms, I was on an observation post with my communications officer and my headquarters commandant, and our fire-support coordination center. Whenever the artillery regiment, the Eleventh Marines, went to Twentynine Palms for a gun shoot, I would request Marine aircraft and take my crew out to practice fire support coordination — orchestrating air and artillery support with infantry.

After we were established on the designated hill, I was called back to Camp Pendleton from Twentynine Palms. While I was at Camp Pendleton, one of drivers of Humvees[9] was out on the desert heading back to the headquarters at Twenty Nine Palms. On the radio he heard that the area where he would soon be driving might be impacted by artillery. So, instead of coming up on the radio and saying, "I'm out here. Check fire until we get this all sorted out," he thought the best thing to do was to speed up his movement across the desert. At this point his Humvee hit a ditch and rolled over. Fortunately, nobody was killed or injured, but the vehicle was damaged.

The accident investigators said, "Well, he shouldn't have raced back. He should have checked in."

I said, "Okay, that's fine, but that's not all." There had been two officers on the observation post during this period of time. I said, "What about them?"

The investigators asked me, "What were they doing wrong?"

"Well," I said, "they were aware of the situation, but didn't take the action that they should have."

My endorsement of the investigation resulted in their receiving what is called a non-punitive letter of caution, which does not go into the record. This action is the mildest form of a wrist-slapping, but it is more than just a chewing-out. It's serious but not career-ending.

I told the investigators, "It doesn't stop there. I also hold myself responsible."

"Well, but you weren't there," they said.

"No," I said. "But I'm still the regimental commander."

So, I wrote a non-punitive letter of caution to myself and took it up to the commanding general to have him sign it.

He looked at it. Then he looked at me. "Draude," he said, "you're crazy."

"No, sir," I said, "This is a matter of accountability. I was accountable even though I wasn't there. I can't hold those two officers accountable without holding myself accountable."

"Well, you'll never make General," the commanding general said.

"That may be, sir," I said, "But this is an opportunity to teach the officers in my regiment a lesson."

"Okay," the commanding general sighed. And he signed off on the letter and told me, "You're a dead man."

I then read to all of the officers of the regiment the non-punitive letter of caution I had written on myself. I used this as an example of what it means to accept accountability, to never put "failure" on the backs of others.

Although I was back at Camp Pendleton when the incident had taken place, I still was accountable for what the regiment accomplished or had failed to accomplish. You don't escape that simply because of distance. Accountability for a leader means you own your mistakes and those of the people you support.

My fault was that I had not instilled in those officers enough accountability so that when they became aware of this incident they would have ordered "Check fire. Wait until we get this thing sorted out." This incident gave me a golden opportunity to demonstrate to the officers in my regiment the importance of accountability. I believe that if you do not accept that as an officer, then it is time to get out. The Marine Corps does not need an officer who thinks he or she can escape accountability simply by not being there.

The Road to Hana

Later in my military career, I had to cope with failing to be promoted from Brigadier General to Major General. I received the message from headquarters while I was assigned as the Assistant Division Commander of the First Marine Division. I joined the division in Saudi Arabia in October 1990. The First Division's focus changed from defensive to offensive in November with the arrival of the Second Marine Division. I spent most of my time on the logistics support of the division as well as assisting in planning artillery raids and the assault into Kuwait. I was designated the deception officer for Marine Forces using amphibious forces, artificial tanks and artillery pieces, and Task Force Troy to achieve surprise and capture Iraqi forces.

When the list of selected Major Generals was published and my name was not on it, people were walking on eggshells around me, fearful of how I would react. So I called my group together—my aide and drivers. I said, "Listen. Let's just clear the air. You know I've been passed over. I know I've been passed over. You had nothing to do with it. It's not your fault. I'm not quitting. This isn't the end of the world. This is just one of those things that happens. I don't want you to feel bad about this or think that things are any different as a result of this taking place. We're all going to be okay, and we have a war ahead of us."

A few months later, the 1st Marine Division had completed all of its training, and we were ready to launch the attack to liberate Kuwait. At this point a message came from Headquarters Marine Corps with the listing of those lieutenant colonels who had been selected for promotion to colonel.

The First Marine Division's commander, General Mike Myatt and I, who was his assistant division commander, discussed the strategy for communicating the news to those within the two affected categories: "good news" for those who had been selected for promotion, and "bad news" for those who had been passed over.

General Myatt and I both wanted to prevent the "bad news" from trickling through the grapevine. We wanted to avoid a dreadful scenario in which those who had not been selected for promotion overheard their fates as they were having a meal or making a head call. Whispers about who was promoted or who was passed over were not the way to hear news like this, as we focused on the battle ahead.

I suggested to Mike, "You tell all of those who've been selected for colonel the good news story. I'll tell all of those who have been passed over for colonel the bad news."

"Well, that's nice of you, Tom," he said. "But why would you separate it that way?"

"Because you've never been passed over. You cannot look a guy in the eye and say, 'I know what you're going through.' I've been passed over and I know how it feels. So, let me do this."

He accepted my recommendation. With that, I summoned my aide, Lieutenant Andrew Harvey, and driver, Sergeant Ferdie

Ingram, and off we went with the list of all the lieutenant colonels who had not been selected to be colonels.

We traversed the entire 1st Marine Division. In some cases, I woke up guys to tell them, "Hey, I want you to hear this from me. You know, this is not the end of the world. But you were not selected for colonel." Although disappointed, all but one took the news in stride. The last officer I visited with the bad news, Lieutenant Colonel Clifford O. (Cliff) Myers III, who was the commanding officer of the 1st Light Armored Infantry Battalion, acted as if I had poleaxed him. He was crushed.

"Good God," I thought to myself, "This cannot be. We can't have a commander going into combat who feels beaten, with his head down and his tail between his legs." After asking God for guidance, I said to Cliff, "Let me tell you a story."

He was not eager for anything more I had to say, but he had no choice other than to listen to my story. Hoping that this would work, I began.

"Years ago," I said, "when I was stationed in Hawaii, on the island of Oahu, my family (Sandi, our three children and Sandi's mother) and I visited Maui. Maui was fantastic! It was fun in the sun with wonderful beaches and all sorts of things to do. However, having read a visitor's brochure that listed "things to do," I suggested taking a trip on the road to Hana.

"The kids resisted with cries of, 'Oh, no, no, we don't want to go! We're having fun here on the beach!'

I reminded them, "Wait a minute – you don't understand. I defend democracy; I don't practice it. So we're going to go to Hana!"

"The next morning, we were up bright and early. The kids and my mother-in-law had long faces, however. The informative brochure suggested bringing lunch and eating it at this beautiful spot halfway through the drive. Because the Draudes usually follow instructions, we bought lunch for our day trip. The attendant who filled the car with gas said that Hana was about 26 miles away and would take about three and a half hours.

Three and a half hours for twenty-six miles? It didn't seem to add up. I figured the attendant was obviously in error. Undeterred, we launched for Hana!

On the winding road were these many one-way bridges, colorful tropical flora, unusual Hawaiian fauna, and all the rest of it. Who cared? Hana was my objective! Halfway across, we took a picture of us eating lunch, but we couldn't eat fast enough because I had to get us to our objective...Hana!

"We got to Hana... 26 miles and three and a half hours later. There was nothing there! Well, almost nothing. Charles Lindbergh and Robert Louis Stevenson are buried there. We traveled all that way to visit the graves of dead guys! I thought this was such a rip-off. I didn't know how they got away with this scam!

"We were gathered in a little 20-by-20-foot courthouse wondering what to do. I happened to look outside and saw two dogs with an obvious romantic interest in each other. And as they were pursuing their manifestations of affection, I turned to Sandi and said, 'We drove all this way to watch a couple of dogs in heat?' The kids all laughed, my mother-in-law got mad, we packed up again, and drove the three-and-a-half hours and 26 miles back to where we started from."

Lieutenant Colonel Myers, still downtrodden, looked up after listening to all of this and said, "So, what's the point?"

"The point, Cliff, is this — we missed it," I said. "See, I got so focused on the objective, Hana, but I forgot to enjoy the beautiful journey. And that's what we often do in life. We get so focused on the objective – ' if I can only make lieutenant colonel,' 'if I can only make colonel,' 'if I get that promotion,' 'if I can only be a supervisor,' 'if I can only get this medal' – we fail to enjoy the journey that got us there — i.e., the family, the friends, the important things."

I continued. "Cliff, we've known each other for a while. Our sons have played baseball together. You're a good husband and father. You're a fantastic Marine. You will be the pointy end of the Division's spear. You're about to make history in the Marine

Corps! Would you trade places with some jerk at Headquarters Marine Corps just because he got selected for colonel?"

He jolted up, "God, no!"

I went on to say, "Appreciate the life you've had. You're about to achieve a whole lot more. But don't get so hung up on the objective, on the destination, that you forget to enjoy the journey. The "Road to Hana" is the point, not Hana."

Lieutenant Colonel Clifford O. Myers went on to receive and combine companies from multiple battalions and to designate the light armored vehicle (LAV) force as Task Force Shepherd. His battalion would be the first in the Marine Corps to use the LAV in combat for reconnaissance and as a tank-killer. The light armored vehicle provided mobility that we previously did not have as infantry. Lieutenant Colonel Myers and his Task Force Shepherd would go on to play a significant role in Operation Desert Storm. And on January 22, 1992, he was selected to the rank of Colonel.

Failure Feels Personal, But It Is Not

Failure is a matter of perception. The journey is the point. Do not become discouraged by the speed bumps or unexpected detours.

In my post-military career, my work was interesting and rewarding but, like countless American workers of all sorts, I was not above the highs and lows of the labor market. In short, I was fired. Twice. Well, actually, once and a half (I'll explain below).

The first time I was fired was when I headed USAA's Tampa regional office. I was attending my Naval Academy class of 1962 40th reunion in Annapolis in 2002. I received a text message to call the home office in San Antonio. We had some claims activities in the region, but nothing unusual or I would have been called by Russ Smith, my Assistant Vice President for claims.

The call was from my boss who sounded hesitant as he informed me that the Property and Casualty line of business (USAA's flagship) was reorganizing and that it would terminate my service as Senior Vice President and General Manager. Up until this time, each regional senior vice president in the Western, Central, Middle Atlantic, and Southeast regions, was held responsible for each region's performance.

One of my delights had been to compete with the other regions, and be held accountable for the results. Now the Region's Vice Presidents – not the Senior Vice Presidents – would be responsible for local community affairs, not the business. Planted between the home office of Property and Casualty would be newly selected "Area Senior Vice Presidents," responsible for two regions each. I was not offered either Vice President of the Tampa office or the Area Senior Vice President.

I informed Sandi of what had transpired, trying to put on a good face as a "new adventure" for us. As usual, she saw right through it as she had when I failed selection for promotion in the Marine Corps. I am grateful to USAA for the opportunity to serve for ten years and to learn more about the challenges of the corporate world while being surrounded by such wonderful employees. USAA continues to be a shining example of quality customer service and prudent financial counseling.

What did I learn? Sometimes candor and taking risks are welcomed and appreciated; sometimes they are not and you pay the price. And sometimes organizations just move in a new direction, without you. Do not take it personally.

My second firing came when I was President and CEO of the Marine Corps University Foundation (MCUF). I accepted the position in 2004, relocating Sandi and our worldly goods to Northern Virginia from Tampa. We had built a home in Lorton, close to my office in Quantico, Virginia. I had a team of superb people, especially retired Lieutenant Colonel John Hales, one of the finest Marines I have ever known.

During the crash of 2008, MCUF fell victim to a Ponzi scheme. Earlier, we had, with unanimous consent of the Board of Trustees, placed our funds with an organization in which one of our trustees worked. It seemed like a good idea to have his eyes on our money. But our trustee and many others were deceived by the leader of this organization.

The bottom line was that I was the leader of the Foundation, which was in trouble. The chairman and some Board members made the decision to fire me. As it turned out, other Board members, led by Guy Wyser-Pratt and Jordan and Tom Sauders, disagreed with my firing and challenged the chairman. The Board decided to retain me as President and CEO and, together, we saved the Foundation. The Foundation today continues to enhance and enrich Professional Military Education and Leadership for students at the Marine Corps University and the operating forces throughout the Marine Corps.

What did I learn from this firing and rehiring? Failure should not produce despair. Somehow, I believed it would all work out despite the initial pain. As leaders, we must be prepared to accept the possibility of being fired for a variety of reasons. We assess the experience and move on in our lives, becoming "better" not "bitter!"

Semper Fs: Figuring Out Failure

- The chance of "failure" is a fact of life, especially for leaders. But leading is worth the risk, since, as I have tried to elucidate, "failure" can also be an opportu- nity for growth. Understanding what led to the mis- take/failure is central to that process. Do not be too quick to judge. What has been learned?

- Rudyard Kipling stated it well in his poem "If": "If you can deal with triumph and disaster, and treat those two imposters just the same...yours is the world, and everything that's in it..." Triumphs and disasters are often, like beauty, in the eye of the beholder. Disasters can become triumphs, and vice versa!

- So much of the progress of humanity is because of failure... and learning from it. Thomas Edison had 1,000 failures before he invented the light bulb. When asked how it felt to fail 1,000 times, he replied, "I didn't fail. The light bulb was an invention with 1,000 steps." Some people are faster learners than others, but success is often the product of failure.

- Remember that FAIL is the acronym for First Attempt In Learning! If there is fear of failure, how do we know what does not work? How will we create more effective alternatives and solutions?

- Not all failures are equal. Some mistakes are lethal, such as producing and marketing a dysfunctional car tire. Leaders can never be casual about health and safety. Encouraging failure doesn't mean abandoning supervision, quality control, or respect for sound practices. Managing failure means that executives are more engaged, not less, in day-to-day operations. Failure-tolerant leaders identify excusable mistakes and approach them as outcomes to be examined, understood, and built upon. They often ask simple but illuminating questions when a project falls short of its goals:

- Was the project designed conscientiously or was it carelessly organized?

Could the failure have been prevented with more thorough research or consultation?

- Distinguishing between excusable and inexcusable mistakes gives leaders a tool to build a nonpunitive environment for making mistakes while encouraging productivity through failure. Leaders promote the sort of productive mistakes that allow all members of the team to learn. New ideas are most likely to emerge in the workplace when leaders treat steps in the innovation process—those that work and those that don't—with objectivity and encouragement.

- Enlightened leaders strive to be collaborative rather than controlling. Failure-tolerant leaders show interest, express support, and ask pertinent questions, e.g.: What's new with your project? What kinds of problems are you having?

Conversations are less about whether the project is succeeding or failing and more about what you can learn from the experience. When leaders and employees are deeply engaged in this discussion, both enter the same kind of high-performance zone that athletes reach when they are operating at their very best. In this zone, evaluation is less relevant than what might be possible next. (A book titled *Flow — The Psychology of Optimal*

Experience (Harper & Row, 1990) by Mihaly Csikszentmihalyi, is worth your time to read.)

- When I reflect back on all the "failures" of my life, I sometimes recall the disappointment and frustration with the undesired outcomes of those situations. However, in retrospect, those "failures" often were the best things that could have happened for me. The key to my realization is time and hindsight. A great quote from the movie, The Best Exotic Marigold Hotel: "Everything will be alright in the end so if it is not alright it is not the end."

---

1. William Childs Westmoreland (1914-2005) was a United States Army general, most notably commander of United States forces during the Vietnam War from 1964 to 1968. He served as Chief of Staff of the U.S. Army from 1968 to 1972. Westmoreland adopted a strategy of attrition against the Viet Cong and the North Vietnamese Army, attempting to drain them of manpower and supplies. Public support for the war eventually diminished, especially after the Battle of Khe Sanh and the Tet Offensive in 1968. By the time he was reassigned as Army Chief of Staff, United States military forces in Vietnam had reached a peak of 535,000 personnel. Westmoreland's strategy was ultimately politically unsuccessful.

2. Westmoreland had disputed the quote in his suit against reporting by CBS. Here is an excerpt from a New York Times article from Nov. 30, 1984: "Gen. William C. Westmoreland and a lawyer for CBS argued yesterday over one of the most memorable phrases of the Vietnam War, with the lawyer suggesting that the general had misled Washington into believing there was "light at the end of tunnel" in 1967 and the general saying he had not used that expression.

   "I never had quite that degree of optimism,' General Westmoreland told the jury at his libel trial against CBS in Federal Court in Manhattan. But the lawyer, David Boies, showed the witness a Nov. 26, 1967, cable he had sent during a visit to Washington to his deputy in Saigon, Gen. Creighton W. Abrams, in which the phrase "some light at the end of the tunnel' was bracketed in quotation marks. Q. Did you believe that degree of optimism was justified? A. I certainly did. I felt it was an accurate and important portrayal."

3. This is now known as the Expeditionary Warfare School (EWS), which provides Marine captains career-level professional military education and oversees their professional military training in command and control.

4. "Golf Company" is a letter company within a battalion. Second battalions in the Marine Corps have companies E, F, and G, aka, Echo, Foxtrot, and Golf per the phonetic alphabet of the military.)

5. During World War II, Dwight D. Eisenhower served as Supreme Commander of the Allied Expeditionary Force in Europe, and achieved the rare five-star rank of General of the Army.

6. George Smith Patton Jr. (1885 – 1945) was a general in the United States Army who commanded the Seventh United States Army in the Mediterranean theater of World War II, and the Third United States Army in France and Germany after the Allied invasion of Normandy in June 1944.

7. Two high-profile incidents of Patton striking subordinates during the Sicily campaign created national controversy. On August 3, 1943, Patton slapped and verbally abused Private Charles H. Kuhl at an evacuation hospital in Nicosia after he had been found to suffer from "battle fatigue" (which is now known as post-traumatic stress syndrome). On August 10, Patton slapped Private Paul G. Bennett under similar circumstances. He ordered both soldiers back to the front lines, railed against cowardice and ordered his commanders to discipline any soldier making similar complaints. Word reached Eisenhower, who privately reprimanded Patton and insisted he apologize. Patton apologized to both soldiers individually, as well as to doctors who witnessed the incidents, and later, in speeches, to all of the soldiers under his command. The incidents became public and criticism of Patton was harsh; it included criticism by members of Congress and former generals.

8. The Judge Advocate General's Corps of the United States Army, also known as the U.S. Army JAG Corps, is the legal arm of the United States Army, established on 29 July 1775 by General George Washington.
9. For "High mobility multipurpose wheeled vehicle."

Part 4 - Feelings

They came at us around 2:00 AM. A Main Force Viet Cong battalion attacked my two platoons on the combat outpost we occupied. We learned later that it was on the resupply route of Viet Cong forces south of us. They meant to kill or capture all of us.

I had anticipated an attack and had registered artillery targets around the hill so we would need only to call in the target we wanted to engage and the US Marine artillery would fire it.

When they hit our lines I reported the situation to battalion and began the request for fire support. Instead, someone decided that what I really needed was an aerial observer and launched a spotter aircraft. Unfortunately, this stopped all artillery support. I shouted to battalion to get the plane out of the area, but to no avail. So we engaged without the support planned.

The next morning we gathered the bodies of the attackers and found on them phonetic cards in English to be used when they captured us. No one was captured, but I lost six Marines in the battle. Their bodies and our wounded were returned to the rear, led by my driver. Any loss is painful and I felt that I could have, should have, done more.

When the driver returned he told my Company Gunnery Sergeant, Gunny Figueroa, what had happened at Graves Registration where my dead Marines were taken. "The Gunny there said to his men, "All right, get these turds (my six dead Marines) off the truck."

I was stunned. How could anyone refer to my Marines as "turds"? These were my Marines. And now some stranger working in the rear whose sole responsibility was to care for our dead refers to them as "Turds"? I was enraged.

I chambered a round in my .45 pistol and ordered my driver to take me to this individual. My blood was up and my only focus at that time was to kill him. All moral rules and restrictions in my life, regardless of faith, military regulations, laws, probable consequences–they all vanished. I had never been so consumed by anger in my life.

Gunny Figueroa saw my anger overcome me and jumped between me and the jeep. "Sir, please don't do this! That guy's just a rear echelon asshole. Forget about him."

"Out of my way, Gunny!" I said. " I'm going to kill this son of a bitch. He's a dead man!"

Gunny grabbed me by the shoulders. "Sir, please don't do this. I'm begging you. If you leave now, we'll never see you again. Then, who will lead us?"

That did it. I came to my senses and regained control of myself. I removed the round from the chamber of my pistol and got back to doing my job leading Mike Company.

I later reflected on how my emotions, my feelings, were so powerful that I almost murdered another Marine. Had it not been for Gunny Figueroa, the rest of my life—marriage, children, grandchildren—would never have happened. Feelings and emotions are ignored at our own peril. We must understand them and the power they can exert over us.

Feelings Mean You Are Human

I was raised in a time when men were not expected to show feelings or sensitivity which could be misinterpreted as "weakness" or sorrow. Men were expected to "suck it up," i.e., take in stride tragedies or setbacks. This was especially true in situations where we were surrounded by other men. My mother once told me that she would be challenged by my dad for being too loving and affectionate toward me as a baby for fear that I would grow up as a "sissy." Mom, thankfully, ignored him! I know my dad loved me in his own way, but he rarely said it or demonstrated signs of affection toward me. I did not feel unloved, but feelings of affection were just not demonstrated among men and boys. So I attempted a stoic posture as a youth.

In my early days Marines had a reputation as hell-raising, cigar-smoking, hard-drinking, jump-off-a-barstool kind of guys who never showed feelings. Because this was not my style, I wonder if I could still be a good Marine?

I learned the answer as a midshipman when I read *Song of the Camp* by James Bayard Taylor about the Crimean War. This poem closes with these words: "The bravest are the tenderest, the loving are the daring." I felt a great relief in this — I could be myself, not copying someone else, and be brave and daring. How a book or poem or movie can change our lives! Marines, as do all humans, have feelings, and leaders are encouraged, at times, to show them.

Feelings play a large role in life and especially in combat. Combat creates a special relationship unlike any other that a Marine will encounter. It is different from friendship, marriage, parenthood, or other bonds. Feelings are powerful tools for a leader on or off the battlefield.

For leaders, combat can play with emotions in cruel ways. That is because as a leader you are expected to accomplish the mission while taking care of your troops. These demands may conflict with each other. To accomplish your mission means risking the lives of those you so deeply care for—your Marines. Training and education and preparation build togetherness and solidarity, but combat can kill without explanation.

When I served in the Marine Corps, we used the phrase "Band of Brothers." It really was. People think that many of these sayings are just recruiting ads. But it's much more than that. You are changed forever when you are in battle with Marines. I am talking about the fear and the affection that military leaders have told us is the key to success. To overcome fear one must have camaraderie, affection and responsibility.

When you become a Marine, you are changed. It is difficult to describe. To this day, when I meet another Marine, whether he or she is on active duty, retired, or served only for a few years, there is a bond. This is a person with whom I feel comfortable and I can trust. Whether he or she was in combat or not is immaterial. This person took a leap of faith and said, "I'm going to go into a dangerous profession. I'm just going to hope for the best and know that I'm going to be surrounded by people like me who are going to get the job done and take care of one another."

Dealing with fear is just a part of being a Marine leader. The responsibilities include not only getting the job done but taking care of your troops. This dual responsibility is far more powerful than fear.

My retrieval of Corporal Miller's body in Vietnam had a powerful impact on all the members of our team. The effect was that there was never a doubt in anybody's mind that a Marine would ever be left behind. At a reunion of Mike Company many years later, one of my Marines was trying to thank me for our time together. I told him that anyone could have done my job because I had such great troops. He stopped, grabbed my arm, looked me in the eye, and said, "Goddammit, sir. Don't you understand? You brought us home!"

Sun Tzu, in *The Art of War*, (Filiquarian Publishing, 2006) wrote, "Regard your soldiers as your children and they will follow you into the deepest valleys. Look on them as your own beloved sons, and they will stand by you even unto death." Those are powerful and accurate words. For those leaders who do always treat those we are privileged to lead as our sons or as our daughters, their 'children' are with them all the way. General John A. LeJeune described relations between an officer and enlisted professionals as being like, "A teacher to scholar...Father to son."

Let me provide a true what-if example. In a rifle company, the command group consists of the commanding officer, the executive officer, first sergeant or gunnery sergeant, a hospital corpsman, and the radio operators. You spend time together and get to know each other very well. Although there is a professional detachment because of rank and position, the command group becomes close.

One of your radio operators, let us say Jonesy, is a fine young American and a selfless Marine. He comes from a loving family which raised him well. You get to know Jonesy – his hometown, the sports he played, the name of his sweetheart, and his plans after serving his time in the Marines. Jonesy is a credit to the company in every way. Then one day you are assaulting an enemy position. Jonesy is at your side, where he always is, and gets hit. You stop long enough for the corpsman to check on him. He tells you, "It's serious, sir." The corpsman wants to medically evacuate Jonesy. Then he says the words that will haunt you forever: "If we don't medevac Jonesy, he's going to die." You know that if you stop the assault to evacuate Jonesy you are risking the lives of the rest of your Marines. So you make that terrible decision to continue the assault.

You might protest that it is not right or fair to be put in a situation where you have to make choices like that. But that's what a leader of Marines must be prepared to do. The feeling of saving a unit conflicts with the feeling of the need to save an individual. Feelings are not always black and white – but they are always with us.

This is why I include feelings as an essential component of the 4Fs of leadership. Feelings arise at every moment of a leader's life.

Feelings affect decision-making, strategy, relationships and more. In this chapter, I am going to explore feelings that leaders confront, in combat situations and in other areas of life. Leadership means sensing where people are succeeding or falling behind. It means having a sense for situations and reading the room or the combat zone. It means realizing people's strengths based on observations and instincts. A feeling can mean the difference between being a cold, distant leader and being an inspiring and engaged one.

I became aware of the profound centrality of feelings to leadership during my second tour in Vietnam. I personally experienced how strong feelings arose out of the close relationships that combat produced. Of course, as is apparent in the scenario above, this means an almost constant tension between caring for individuals while also being responsible for the entire unit.

There are going to be times when, as a leader, your feelings are just going to tear you apart, but you cannot show them. You have to be that stoic person who stays focused on the mission because if you do not you are going to cause other people to be maimed or killed. Those feelings will come out later.

There must be a balance. You do not want to get so hung up on casualty aversion that you avoid doing what has to be done, but you do what has to be done with the thought of not wasting any lives. This balance and tension affected me throughout my military career.

My friend Bill Griffis was an advisor with me, and we had been together at Amphibious Warfare School and the Marine Advisor Course. In 1970, I was on a rest and relaxation (R&R) break spent in Hawaii with Sandi. (We had two children at the time who were in Buffalo with her parents.) It was a wonderful time together. However, as soon as I arrived at the airport in Saigon awaiting transport to return to duty, a friend of mine met me to tell me that Bill had been killed.

Normally, after R&R, you received a couple of days in Saigon to decompress before returning to duty. But I felt that I needed to get back out into the field with my Vietnamese Marines.

I had to be able to focus on those whom I could save in order to accomplish the mission. In this case I was aware of the importance of what my unit, the 5th Battalion Vietnamese Marines, was doing. They needed me in the Delta with them. They did not need me in Saigon sitting in a hotel room feeling bad for Bill Griffis. There was nothing I could do for Bill, but I could do something for the Vietnamese Marines. Later there would be time to reflect and mourn and go through those feelings. Much later, I had the solemn honor of telling Bill's two grown daughters about the father they never knew. His younger daughter, Mitty, was born about the time he was killed. She was now a television reporter with a cool, professional demeanor. But when I told her that the last entry in her dad's notebook was, "It's due today," meaning his wife Sally was scheduled to give birth to her, Mitty became the sorrowful daughter who realized one of her dad's last thoughts was of her, the daughter he never saw or held.

I think sometimes of the kind of impact I had on the Vietnamese Marines with whom I served. I believe it was positive. When my tour was over, we were in Cambodia just after our incursion in 1970. One of the Vietnamese lieutenants, who had just come back from the United States where he had gone to the Marine Corps Basic School, said something that meant the world to me. He said, "Because of you, many lives were saved." He knew of a time when I had gone through a minefield to retrieve a wounded Vietnamese Marine in order to medevac him to safety. "I know of the wonderful way of life in the United States," he said, "the wealth, the luxuries, the pleasures — the things that are a part of the United States. To think that you would give up all of that and possibly your own life for me and my people is just amazing. Thank you for what you've done."

I never forgot those words. I was both humbled and honored by them. We were sacrificing a great deal. We were Marines. I understood intimately all those things that President John F. Kennedy spoke about: "We shall pay any price, bear any burden…to assure the survival and success of liberty."

The Best Leaders Feel Empathy

In my career, empathy and perspective have played large parts. When I used to talk to Marines about being an advisor or trainer, I always began by saying, "Not every good Marine or soldier or airman or sailor could be a good advisor or trainer." That's because this role requires two things that you cannot fake. You have to like the people with whom you're working and you must have patience. With both the Vietnamese and, later, with the Saudis, that was absolutely the case.

At the time of Desert Storm, I worked with the Saudis, and in particular, a Colonel Turki,[1] Commander of the Second Brigade, Saudi Arabian National Guard, with whom I had built a relationship.[2] It began when he stepped off a helicopter to meet me for the first time and I greeted him with *Salaam Alaikum*, peace be unto you. He seemed startled that an American could speak Arabic. In fact, this was most of the Arabic I knew!. Later, I visited him, sipped tea with him and watched what he was doing. That was because it was necessary to get both of us at ease in working with each other and learning from each other. Like me, serendipitously, General Mike Myatt and General Walt Boomer, the MEF Commander, had been advisors in Vietnam, as had Colonel John Admire,[3] the regimental commander who was going to be working with the Saudis. So, I didn't have to spend time convincing any of them of how important it was to have these relationships and to get involved with the intermingling of the units.

When one works in an advisory capacity on foreign soil, the first barrier is language. Most Marines did not speak Arabic and many of the Saudi soldiers spoke no or very little English. But with feeling, empathy, and respect, we were able to get through the challenge that speaking different languages presented.

I saw our Marines and Saudi National Guardsmen disassemble weapons in their own languages or a combination of the two languages, but they were able to communicate. The Saudi's were learning from us things such as tactics, weapons, and so forth. We were learning from them things such as land navigation, which is certainly a tremendous challenge in the desert, as well as how to simply live safely in the desert. It began with mutual respect and admiration; we were willing to spend time together, and to have our forces involved in training with their forces. As a result of this type of cooperation, we were able to accomplish most of our goals.

This all paid off in the Battle of Khafji,[4] which is one of the battles that preceded our actual invasion into Kuwait. The Battle of Khafji is where the Iraqis invaded and captured the northernmost town in Saudi Arabia for a day or so. After they had attacked and seized the town, Colonel Turki got the order from his higher headquarters, "Attack Khafji and retake it." As Colonel Turki was planning his assault, Colonel Admire came to his headquarters and said, "Colonel Turki, I'm here to inform you that whatever you need from the U.S. is yours."

Colonel Turki responded, "The Marines are with us — we attack!"

With the support of Marine artillery and some of the reconnaissance units and others, the Saudi's retook Khafji. The Battle of Khafji was significant because it did two things. It dispelled the notion that the Iraqi soldier was "ten-feet tall, a superb soldier with so much combat experience." While Iraq had the fourth-largest land Army in the world, and although Iraqis had been fighting the Iranians for eight years, they started shrinking rapidly. Secondly was the realization that the Saudis were ready and willing to fight.

Every part of these interactions involved feelings – trust, confidence, and enthusiasm – that are rarely identified, but that play a huge role in decision-making. Creating a relationship with the Saudis was very important in the success of our missions.

I used my military logistics experience – and my empathy – on more than a few occasions during my civilian career. One note-worthy instance occurred when I was a senior vice president at USAA Federal Savings Bank. We were moving our very profitable credit card operations from Tulsa, Oklahoma, to our home office in San Antonio, Texas. I volunteered to head the team that would deal with the logistics of this move.

This move was more than physical. It was essential that people in Tulsa were aware of everything that was going on, and that we treated them with respect and gratitude, because their jobs were at stake.

To begin with, as we were organizing the move, I flew every two weeks to Tulsa with my team to deal with on-the-ground preparations and also to meet the people in the Tulsa operation. I wanted to get to know these people. I wanted to make sure we were putting into action the adage, "You can pretend to care but you can't pretend to be there."

As always, I was thinking about how to make this transition easy and smart. Not only were we moving the operation but also, potentially, a lot of people who we needed to join us in San Antonio. For example, I met with a national credit-card processing company, FDR, that had partnered with us so that when our credit card operations were being moved, FDR would fill the gap.

I spoke to the Tulsa team using non-military terms that would make sense to them, given most did not have a military background, even though they worked at a company whose members had military connections. One of the Human Resources (HR) executives at USAA advised me that employees' expectations are that good news is delivered with food and bad news gets only beverages. I made sure we provided sandwiches and pastries along with the coffee, and soft drinks.

I began by first thanking everyone there for what they had done for USAA, to make the credit card center such a success. I then outlined the choices they would have. If they decided to leave USAA as a result of this move, they would be offered a generous severance package and receive excellent recommendations. If they were to consider staying with the company and moving to San Antonio, but wanted to check it out first, we would offer them a day trip to San Antonio to look around the neighborhoods, check out the school districts, etc. There were no obligations. For those who wanted to stay in Tulsa, they had the option to continue to work for the credit card center that would then be taken over by FDR. The employees who selected this option would remain at the same salaries and with the same position; the only thing that would change would be the logo on the door. Finally, if they decided to move to San Antonio, USAA would provide a loan that would allow them to buy their first home there.

We hoped that perhaps 10% of leadership would transfer to San Antonio, but in fact over 50% of the Tulsa leaders and more than 20% of the other employees decided to come with us to San Antonio! As for our USAA members, we wanted them to see no decline in service. Everything ran smoothly as it always had, even though our physical headquarters had moved.

This transition was a success because we thought in terms of the feelings of the Tulsa employees and placed ourselves in their situation. We wanted to assure them they would still be valued, regardless of their decisions. In all, these instances of feelings, from the battlefield to the boardroom, have been essential leadership qualities.

You Can Pretend to Care, But You Cannot Pretend to Be There

One of the most important parts of leadership is showing up. You can be eloquent and you can be brilliant and possess all the rest of the attributes that leaders are supposed to have, but if you are not present, you send a worrisome signal. Whether it's in combat or in peacetime the leaders need to be where they can see and be seen. Their presence is extremely important, especially in desperate times. Subordinates must know that the person in charge is present doing what has to be done, and understands intimately what's happening on the ground. This is absolutely critical for success.

While I served with USAA, when there was any sort of catastrophe, we would dispatch teams of both claims people and policy service personnel to the affected area. The policy service personnel were good at listening. People who had been through a disaster needed to tell their stories before they got into the details of what was lost and how to replace it. Policy service personnel listened to their stories as a key first step. Once the members shared their experiences, it was easier for the claims people to do their job of settling the claim. Part of it also was to be aware of lessons to be learned, not repeated, and actions that should result in recognition or awards. These are all the follow-on things that are often forgotten or not mentioned, but are necessary not just in combat but also in emergencies in civilian leadership. People need to feel they are heard and seen, and the best way to support them as a leader is to be with them and to listen.

Semper Fs: Feelings are Fundamental

- Leaders need to know when to allow themselves to expose their feelings and when they need to compartmentalize them. This is not hypocrisy. All of us learn when and where to let our feelings show. Choose carefully — your actions as a leader are always being observed.

- Empathy allows leaders to better understand the feelings of those in their units which can help in motivating them. People will feel more valued and heard when leaders acknowledge and understand the feelings and experiences of those they lead.

- The best leaders are able to hit a pause button when they become emotional. Instead of immediately reacting, they ask themselves, "What exactly am I feeling? Why? What is the need or fear behind this emotion?" For example, average leaders might say they feel irritable about a project because the workload is annoying, but stronger leaders will take the time to reflect on this emotion, examining its origins. In doing so, they might realize the root cause of their irritability is anxiety about meeting a deadline, for example.

- Address your feelings. If you are frustrated or upset, your employees most likely will pick up on your bad mood and might assume that they are responsible for it. (Do not let the inconsiderate driver who cut you off on your way to work ruin the whole day for you and your followers!) Acknowledging your feelings helps you avoid creating unnecessary anxiety among the members of your team.

- Provide a path forward. When you are tackling a challenging project, practice how you are going to share your emotions with your team members, and make sure you do so with the proper intention. Dumping your feelings onto them in a reactive or unthoughtful way leaves too much room for misinterpretation. Aim to be realistic but optimistic. (Remember Napoleon: "Leaders are dealers in hope!")

- Read the room. If you think members of your team might be feeling anxious about a project, it is okay to address those feelings. For example, if everyone has been working long hours to meet an impending deadline, you might say something like, "I'm sensing that we're all feeling a bit tired today. But I'm grateful for how well we've worked together and that we're set to send the client a proposal that makes us proud."

- Our inspiration is often the result of not just what we hear or see, but how we feel. What inspires you to become better? What can you do to inspire others to become better? Is there a word or a gesture that can be offered? Is your presence needed? When I headed the USAA office in Tampa, before we instituted "extended hours" to provide assistance 24/7, the Tuesday after a long weekend could be brutal. It was as if Tuesday after a Monday holiday was like a "double Monday morning!" I instituted in our cafeteria a "Drinks on Draude" program so that fountain beverages and coffee were free on those days. It was not much, but it was a way of showing appreciation for working through a tough day. On these double Mondays, we also made sure all our leaders were present in our work spaces, demonstrating their appreciation to all employees.

---

1. "When it became clear that the 1st Marine Division would be fighting beside Saudi forces, the division's commander, Major General James M. Myatt, ordered his assistant division commander, Brigadier General Tomas V. Draude, to take primary responsibility for liaison duties. Brigadier

General Draude used 3d Marines, the Marine unit nearest to Joint Forces Command-East units, as the primary focus of his liaison effort." – from U.S. Marines in Battle – Al-Khafji, 28 January – 1 February 1991, by Paul W. Westermeyer, 2008, History Division United States Marine Corps Washington, D.C.

2. "The largest Marine unit in the area was Task Force Taro. Its extensive cross training efforts with the Saudi National Guard brigade under Colonel Turki had created a bond between the two units..." – from "U.S. Marines in the Persian Gulf, 1990-1991 – With the 1st Marine Division in Desert Shield and Desert Storm," by Lieutenant Colonel Charles H. Cureton U.S. Marine Corps Reserve, History and Museums Division Headquarters, U.S. Marine Corps Washington, D.C., 1993.

3. John H. Admire is a retired U.S. Marine major general. Admire is a decorated veteran of the Vietnam War and previously served as commanding general of 1st Marine Division.

4. The Battle of Khafji was the first major ground engagement of the Gulf War. It took place in and around the Saudi Arabian city of Khafji, from January 29 January to February 1, and marked the culmination of the Coalition's air campaign over Kuwait and Iraq, which had begun on January 17 that year.

Wrapping Up the 4Fs

Mark Twain said, "The two most important days in your life are the day you were born and the day you found out why."

That second day for me was when I was in first grade and our teacher, Sister Ann Dominic, announced we needed to elect a class president. Her challenge somehow appealed to me. I am not sure what attracted me more, the power or prestige or to be able to correct things...to get things right.

After that, I was elected class president for every year through high school. I believe I was class president so often because I volunteered to serve. There were not a lot of "office seekers" in those days!

It became natural for me to volunteer to lead. My dream of becoming a Marine carried with it the dream of leading Marines. I became a student of leadership and remain one to this day. I am amazed at all the books, videos, articles, etc., on leadership. I can see why some youngsters find it daunting to learn leadership with so much material available. That is why I love and use what Douglas S. Freeman said at the Naval War College as a structure for my talks on leadership.*

My life in the Marines shaped my views of leadership and gave me great insights into working with people. I have shared with you within these pages my experiences such as they apply to leadership in all of the four "F" forms I have identified: fatigue, fear, failure, and feelings.

Leadership means much more than these four qualities, but each of my "F's" encompasses a great deal of what leaders face during their careers. Leadership should be a shared experience based on a life lived with purpose. As you reflect on your own leadership journey, ask yourself, who or what will be better, because of you? What is your purpose? Why were you born?

My hope is that my thoughts in this book will assist you in being a leader who makes a difference.

Semper Fidelis!

---

* "Know your stuff; be a person of character; take care of your people.

Acknowledgments

The structure of the "Four Fs" was the idea of my daughter Loree and our comrade Bob Hughes, based on the talk I gave to Marines about engaging in combat before Desert Storm in 1991. Of tremendous assistance were my Goddaughter Melissa Manzanares and Kelly Crager of Texas Tech University's Center for Vietnamese studies. Both conducted extensive interviews with probing questions of me. Those interviews form the basis of this book. I am deeply indebted to them as well as to Loree, Cari Costanzo and Fred Rainbow, all of whom edited my manuscript, which was much required and appreciated!

My wife Sandi and sons Patrick and Ryan are the rest of my immediate family. They have been and continue to be members of my "leadership laboratory," giving constant support and feedback. They also have been major factors in whatever success I've enjoyed. Their love has been constant and unwavering and they are my role models. Every move was an adventure because Sandi made it so. Our children grew up accepting a move every

one, two, or three years as normal, leaving behind close friends. When the new orders arrived, Sandi, a superb teacher, would start her logistics miracle as she continued to teach. It was unfair that when we moved there was a position waiting for me, an assigned mission, an office and sometimes even a parking space! Sandi, who had risen to the top at her previous school, had to start all over again. She never complained!

I also treasure the friendship of my dearest friend, General Chuck Krulak, 31st Commandant of the Marine Corps. I first met Chuck when we were at the Naval Academy as midshipmen. He was two years behind me. It was the only time he's been behind me! He always has been the leader or comrade of those blessed to know him. We served together at Amphibious Warfare School as captains, Headquarters Marine Corps, the National War College, and Headquarters Fleet Marine Force, Pacific as lieutenant colonels, and in Desert Storm as brigadier generals. He has been instrumental in so many good things in my professional and personal life. He is truly a brother to me.

Finally, I thank God for the many blessings my family and I have received. I am the luckiest person alive!

www.ingramcontent.com/pod-product-compliance
Lightning Source LLC
Chambersburg PA
CBHW070235220526
45465CB00004B/1425